THE
MAD GENIUS
CONTROVERSY

SOCIOLOGICAL OBSERVATIONS

series editor: JOHN M. JOHNSON, *Arizona State University*

·····●●●·····

"This new series seeks its inspiration primarily from its subject matter and the nature of its observational setting. It draws on all academic disciplines and a wide variety of theoretical and methodological perspectives. The series has a commitment to substantive problems and issues and favors research and analysis which seek to blend actual observations of human actions in daily life with broader theoretical, comparative, and historical perspectives. SOCIOLOGICAL OBSERVATIONS aims to use all of our available intellectual resources to better understand all facets of human experience and the nature of our society."

—John M. Johnson

Volumes in this series:

THE
MAD
GENIUS
CONTROVERSY

A Study in the Sociology of Deviance

George Becker

SAGE Publications   Beverly Hills   London

For information address:

SAGE PUBLICATIONS, INC.
275 South Beverly Drive
Beverly Hills, California 90212

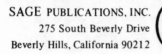

SAGE PUBLICATIONS LTD
28 Banner Street
London EC1Y 8QE

Printed in the United States of America

Library of Congress Cataloging in Publication Data

Becker, George.
   The mad genius controversy.

   (Sociological observations ; v. 5)
   Bibliography: p.
   Includes index.
   1. Deviant behavior. 2. Genius. I. Title.
II. Series.
HM291.B375   301.6'2   78-875
ISBN 0-8039-0985-3
ISBN 0-8039-0986-1 pbk.

FIRST PRINTING

Contents

To Janet and Gregory

Acknowledgments

Few books are written without a share of indebtedness. This one is no exception. Many people generously donated time, thoughts, experience and, as in the case of my wife, great measures of patience and understanding as well.

Lewis A. Coser listened to the initial thought, suggested ways to formulate the project and was, in fact, the source of consistent scholarly and friendly guidance from the first dull glimmer of the idea to the finished book. His support and assistance has been central to my efforts, and his offer to write a Foreword is greatly appreciated.

Others, like John H. Gagnon, Kai T. Erikson, James Rule, Forrest Dill, Werner T. Angress, Erich Goode, and Robert Stevenson took time to read the manuscript in various stages of completion and offered valuable advice. Kai T. Erikson, in particular, was exhaustive in his response, and many of his suggestions will be incorporated in future work.

Special mention also must go to Stewart Forde, who spent long hours in editing the manuscript with an eye not only for correctness of expression, but for clarity of ideas as well. And Anne McGovern must be thanked for her hours of work in providing content analysis of the French sources.

Finally, no words are sufficient to acknowledge my indebtedness to Janet Becker, my wife—an inexhaustible worker and a constant source of energy and optimism. While working full time in her own career, she did all of the typing, much of the editing, and was extremely helpful in discussing the ideas found in this work.

Foreword
by Lewis A. Coser

It seems inevitable that academic disciplines become subject to a process of differentiation after they have succeeded in elaborating a peculiar
approach that distinguishes them from neighboring fields, and after
their activities have become institutionally validated. While the founders
of a discipline might still claim to encompass the whole field, their suc-
cessors typically cultivate a narrower area. In the nineteenth century,
historians, for example, were drawn mostly to universal investigations
or at least claimed long stretches of historical time as their domain. In
contrast, modern historians have become specialized. They are Euro-
peanists or Americanists, eighteenth-century scholars or economic
historians. Similarly in sociology, a Durkheim, a Simmel, or a Max
Weber roamed freely in space and time in search of valid sociological
knowledge and needed no excuse for lecturing on religion in one
semester and on urban phenomena in the next. Contemporary sociologists, however, are social demographers, social psychologists,
methodologists, criminologists, or the like.

Such a development is no doubt unavoidable. The growth of knowledge, the proliferation of research methods and findings make it impossible for any individual to encompass a whole general area; it forces
those who wish to make a major contribution to concentrate attention
on a limited field of investigations. Yet, there always lurks the danger
that excessive compartmentalization leads to a kind of tower of Babel,
where the various practitioners in the subfields have lost the capacity to
understand one another and to profit from findings that did not ema-
nate in their own field. While specialization and differentiation seem
indeed necessary in mature or maturing disciplines, excessive specialization stultifies growth in as far as it inhibits communication between
areas and fosters a kind of inbreeding that ultimately must result in
sterility.

This being the case, balance growth of an overall discipline, although dependent on specialized work, also needs the contribution of scholars who have the capacity to transcend narrow boundaries of specialization, and the ability to translate the findings or approaches of one discipline or subdiscipline into the language of the other. Without scholars who perform such bridging functions the necessary dialogue between different specialties threatens to become a dialogue of the deaf.

It is the distinct merit of George Becker's *The Mad Genius Controversy* that it performs such a needed bridging function. Putting to good uses his earlier training in the field of history and his wide reading in historical sociology, Becker chose to deal with a problem suggested by contemporary labeling approaches, which hitherto had been applied almost exclusively to contemporary data. He uses guidelines from labeling theory in the investigation of a problem in historical sociology, and thereby illuminates a crucial area that is of relevance not only to the sociology of knowledge but also to cultural sociology broadly conceived.

"A person becomes the thing he is described as being," wrote Frank Tannenbaum, the first and now almost forgotten formulator of a labeling approach to the study of deviance. If that be so, argues George Becker, what were the causes and consequences of the fact that in the last half of the nineteenth century, a great variety of intellectuals were labeled as madmen by an array of respectable medical practitioners and other persons who claimed a scientific warranty for their negative appraisal of the worth and sanity of men of genius? Analyzing in instructive detail the complicated dialectic relations between intellectuals in general and artistic creators in particular, and those scientists who pretended to be able to judge their mental states, Becker shows that it would be simplistic to see this process as an imposition of negative labels on passive victims. He documents that during the Romantic period intellectuals and artists developed idiosyncratic types of behavior that were meant to distinguish them from the common herd. But at a later stage, these deviant behavioral styles in turn provided the basis and the raw materials for the stereotyped labels of those who had a vested interest in their own construction of the image of the "mad genius." Hence many a Romantic "genius," actuated by the need for an affirmed identity that stressed his "otherness," helped initiate a process in which others took him more seriously than he perhaps wished, and assigned him to the status of a madman. Their own assumption of a deviant life-style rendered the Romantic writers and artists and their descendants defenseless against the label of madness. Those who did the labeling, to be sure, were intent largely upon defending the received verities and status quo assumptions against new winds of doctrine propagated by "subversive" intellectuals, but they were able to do so because their victims had largely prepared the groundwork for them.

There is no need in this short introduction to follow the intricacies of Becker's analysis, or the subtle distinctions through which he succeeds in showing what type of persons were to be found in the ranks of the labelers and the labeled. All this the reader can readily discern for himself. I only wish to stress here that Becker's result, while refining and modifying theory through historical investigation, has at the same time largely succeeded in illuminating a problem that has continued to puzzle a number of cultural historians.

My former colleague, Everett C. Hughes, used to ask his graduate students after they had successfully defended their thesis, "What other areas of sociological knowledge over and beyond the one you have investigated might profit from your findings?" Had Becker been one of those students he would have been able to reply with some confidence that such areas as the sociological study of prejudice, of race relations, or of antisemitism might be studied profitably by the same method. By throwing light upon an apparently limited area of historical and cultural experience, Becker has given other scholars conceptual handles to investigate other aspects of the vast canvas of human social phenomena. And this, I would submit, is the measure of his success.

—Lewis A. Coser
State University of New York
at Stony Brook

Introduction

The relation of genius to madness has been a subject of controversy in Western society since the start of the Romantic Movement. Prior to this time the prevailing conception of the genius, while recognizing certain subrational components, saw him as essentially sane and rational. The Romantics redefined the genius, downgrading rational components and bringing irrationality into the foreground. During the mid-nineteenth century, fueled by this redefinition, the developing mental health movement advanced "scientific" evidence underscoring the association of genius with various forms of mental illness. While for subsequent decades this judgment enjoyed a majority consensus, it nevertheless unleashed in various disciplines polemics that collectively comprise the body of the mad genius controversy. This dispute reached in certain cases an emotional intensity, as Lange-Eichbaum (1935:16) observed, reminiscent of a "Glaubenskrieg" or conflict of ideologies. Indeed, this high degree of emotional involvement appeared inevitable given the nineteenth century's fascination with hero worship and the cult of genius.

The issue of genius and madness—debated for roughly a hundred years—is not only of deep historical concern, but suggests itself as a challenge to the sociological study of deviance. The change in the dominant conception of genius from "sane" to "mad" offers on opportunity to explore the dynamics of labeling as they apply, not only to select individuals, but to an entire category of persons—the men of genius. The treatment of the mad genius controversy as a sociological phenomenon permits focusing on the issue of "causes" or determinants of negative typing. This study examines historical, social, and intellectual changes responsible for the redefinition of genius; in addition, it will attempt an evaluation of the common use of the existing labeling paradigm in sociology.

The application of a sociological perspective to a historical problem poses certain difficulties. Most importantly, there is a tendency to slight or oversimplify the complexity of historical processes. In an attempt to transcend the realm of historical specificity and to search for generalized types, the sociological approach fails to capture the uniqueness and rich texture of historical developments. Its greatest compensating attribute, however, is its ability to provide a framework for grasping relationships among complex phenomena. The labeling perspective, as one sociological approach, provides such a framework.

The factor that distinguishes the labeling orientation from other perspectives in the sociology of deviance is that it has been used to shift attention away from the traditional focus upon rule-violators toward the societal reaction to these rule-violators.[1] Instead of locating the source of deviance in the rule-breaker, the labeling orientation purports to see the deviant, and those who label him as such, in a complementary relationship where one cannot exist without the other. Viewed from this standpoint, deviance is not an individual flaw as much as it is a result of a social process that involves conflicting values or expectations of social groups, social reactions, the role of third parties, and cultural rules on typing. Having redefined the problem of deviance in this way, one important implication for research is that the defining agents (or labelers) and agencies of social control become a subject for study. Accordingly, the focal questions are how, why and with what consequences do certain groups define given behaviors as deviant, immoral, or criminal, and subsequently judge those so defined as requiring treatment, control, or punishment?

When applied to that form of deviance that we identify by the term "mental illness," the labeling approach involves what Thomas Scheff (1974) calls a "social system model" of mental illness. Unlike the traditional "medical" or "individual system" models, which focus on individual differences, the social system model concentrates on the social environment in which the individual operates and the attendant social contingencies responsible for labeling the individual as mad. The factor that warrants the treatment of mental illness as a sociological concern is the realization that the prevalence of "abnormal" psychiatric symptoms in ostensibly normal populations is exceedingly high. In fact, the evidence suggests that the number of untreated cases with "abnormal" psychiatric symptoms may indeed by higher than the cases receiving treatment (Scheff, 1974:47-51). This apparent selectivity of identification inheres in the societal reaction. Faced with the deviation from rules in their immediate social environment, people have a number of options available to them. They may ignore or rationalize rule violations as a special case of normal behavior; they may make accommodations that obscure the violations; they may draw attention to violations and even exaggerate the nature of these. Given these options, central questions arise for the sociologist. Why are certain individuals selected and typed "mad," but not others? What social, historical, or intellectual contingencies predispose or facilitate this discrimination? Indeed, are some individuals or groups of individuals more susceptible to typing? And if so, what accounts for this?

With regard to the mad genius controversy one approach simply would be to accept the notion that men of genius are indeed a pathological stock and to proceed from this assumption. Another would be to ascribe to all men of genius an extraordinary sensitivity to their environment, a sensitivity that results in abnormal perceptions and behavior.[2] However, the position that is most consistent with the labeling perspective is to adopt what has been called an "agnostic" stance. This position enables the investigator to describe patterns of symptoms, treatments, and beliefs pertaining to mental illness without having to endorse or reject them himself. Indeed, as Scheff (1967:10) observes, even the key assumption regarding mental illness in modern Western society, namely that it constitutes a disease or illness, could become a point of investigation. Freed from the clinical preoccupation with the individual, the researcher is enabled to pursue a variety of the larger social issues related to mental illness.

On the most general level, this study seeks to ascertain which pivotal developments or changes in Western culture were responsible for the transformation of the once-prevailing conception of genius. This general scope of inquiry suggests itself in view of the fact that we are dealing, not merely with isolated cases subjected to negative typing, but with an entire category of individuals. It seems clear that a major redefinition of status for a category of men could be effected only as a result of some unique combination of developments. Indeed, an overview of Western history suggests that the mad genius polemics were conducted in an atmosphere permeated by change and upheaval—an age characterized by the advent of industrialization, urbanization, and mass democracy, the rise of conflicting world views, and changes in taste and artistic expression. Clearly, the failure to take account of key social, political, and intellectual developments could lead to serious distortions in the interpretation of the phenomenon at hand. However, to attempt a comprehensive historical account of these changes is not within the scope of this study. The explicit focus pertains to the process of labeling and the criteria specific to the imputation of mental illness. This decision dictates, more or less, that the primary source of data for this investigation becomes that body of literature written on genius and the issue of madness. This in no way should mean that a sociological inquiry of this type must remain insensitive to large-scale changes in Western society. In fact, the very focus on these monographs cannot leave the impact of these changes obscured. The individuals involved in the mad genius debate were, to a large degree, products of their age—in the sense that they employed in their writings intellectual concepts and categories current in that time and served as the spokesmen on behalf of ideas, aspirations, fears, and sentiments particular to their age. While a content analysis of these materials cannot permit the construction of a historically detailed picture describing the changes in the sociocultural realm, it can serve, nevertheless, to underscore the effects of these changes as they pertained to the genius controversy. Unable, for instance, to provide a historical account of the changing social position of the man of genius (man of letters, artist, and so forth), this approach is ideally suited for determining whether the man of genius was perceived as threatening and, if so, for what reasons. Similarly, while it is not possible to trace the intellectual history of the times, it may be ascertained whether changing conceptions of man, mind, and mental illness were instrumental in the redefinition of genius, short of providing a genesis of these changes. It is in their relation to the redefinition of genius that the nature of the changes in the sociocultural realm can be assessed.

As indicated, a defining characteristic of the labeling perspective is its assumption that deviance should be conceived not so much as rule-breaking conduct, but as the consequence of rule-making and the selective application of such rules. In this view, the relation of the "deviant" to his labeler is regarded as crucial. Unlike those situations where the labeler and labeled are contemporaries and engage in more or less direct interaction, the mad genius controversy quite frequently centered on exceptional individuals already deceased. While it is impossible, therefore, to examine the interactive process involving both "deviant" and labeler, the time problem, when it exists, does not preclude viewing the relationship of the "deviant" to his labeler complementarily. Proceeding from the basic assumption of the labeling perspective that rule-making and the enforcement of rules are selective processes that often reflect self-serving purposes, this study seeks to discern the degree to which the label of "mad" might have served as a means of social control. While it is clear that many of the individuals so labeled were deceased, and therefore not subject to direct coercion, intellectual and creative products remain subject to continued evaluation. Viewed in this light, the imputation of madness to the deceased could serve to discredit not only contemporary individuals, but also particular ideas and schools of thought. In cases where the concept of mad was applied to most or all geniuses, labeling can be seen as an attempt to discredit the social category of genius.

With regard to the individuals typed, a distinction must be drawn between the "mad" and "sane" men of genius. This follows from the fact that even in the negative assessments of genius (where defined as pathological), the existence of certain "sane" geniuses was generally noted. The basic question then arises as to what distinguished the sane geniuses from those judged to be mad. One approach that will be adopted is the examination of the intellectual activity in which the genius engaged. Specifically, individuals will be distinguished on the basis of categories such as poet, painter, mathematician, philosopher, and so forth. From this, it becomes possible to discern to what degree various intellectual endeavors have been identified with mental pathology. A second approach is to deal with the evaluation of given intellectual products. Accordingly, it can be asked whether an unfavorable assessment of a piece of art, philosophy, or criticism on the part of the labeler predisposes him to negative typing. Conversely, is a "sane" genius one whose intellectual product is favorably received? A final approach is to compare the "mad" with the "sane" geniuses on the basis of their presumed adherence to specific behaviors, values, norms, beliefs, and attitudes. It should be noted that, consistent with the theoretical requirement of the problem, all evaluations about so-called men of genius will be based on the information provided by the labelers. While the consultation of additional materials should provide more reliable portrayals of these men, the main concern of this study deals with labeling and the criteria specific to such labeling.

In order to explore the question of motivation on the part of the labelers, it is not entirely sufficient to confine the investigation to the appropriate monographs on genius. Because not all authorities supported the generally presumed association of genius and madness, it becomes necessary to distinguish the "dissenters" from those who endorsed the presumed relationship. Such a comparison can be conducted purely on the basis of the evaluative statements made about men of genius. However, even the addition of basic biographical information, allowing a breakdown of these two groups of individuals in general terms of profession and educational background, will serve to elucidate the issue of motivation in labeling.

Finally, it must be noted that this study departs from the usual concerns of the users of the labeling perspective in two ways. First, while the perspective ordinarily is concerned with the labeling process itself and its immediate causes, this paper considers certain changes of widely held fundamental attitudes and their effect on the labeling of geniuses. These changes, it will endeavor to show, made virtually inevitable the association of genius with madness. Indeed, the inevitability of associating madness with genius, given developments and changes of widely held attitudes, is the organizing idea of this study; specific observations on genius and its labeling will take place within this context. Second, while the employers of the labeling perspective have been concerned primarily with the labeler, data in this study reflects that negative labeling is often self-initiated.[3] It is hoped, therefore, that this study, while using the labeling perspective, will be able to take into consideration factors beyond the usual scope of its concern, and therefore provide a picture of the mad genius controversy that will transcend certain limitations of the usual use of a labeling perspective.

NOTES

1. In the study of deviance and social control, the labeling framework is also known, often with slight differences in meaning, as the social control model, societal reaction model or interactionist model. It should be noted that in this description of the labeling framework the term "theory" is consciously being avoided. The labeling perspective is not treated here as a theory in the formal sense, but as a framework, orientation, or sensitizing device (see E. Goode, 1975). This framework is best exemplified in the works of Howard S. Becker (1963, 1967), Edwin Lemert (1951, 1967), and Thomas Scheff (1967, 1974).

2. e.g., Morse Peckham (1970) conceives of geniuses as victims of a culture crisis who are driven to illness by perceived contradictions in the social order.

3. When the focus is on the labeled, it is generally in terms of victimization and identity management.

Relating Genius and Madness

An Historical Overview

The genesis of an idea or concept frequently has decisive importance for its subsequent development. This is particularly true with the idea of genius. The "modern" conception of genius—as the manifestation of the highest form of innate original ability in individuals—first received popularization during the eighteenth century. Etymologically, the term has its roots in antiquity. While the modern conception of genius is quite different from the classical use of the term, its indebtedness to antiquity is apparent in the retention of a markedly mystical component. This semireligious quality surrounding the notion of genius constitutes a cornerstone in the association of genius with madness. This chapter will sketch the development of the genius concept from its origin in antiquity to the present and will relate this development to the issue of madness. Specifically, it will seek to demonstrate that the association of genius with clinical insanity, while foreshadowed in earlier times, did not become firmly established until the end of the nineteenth century, from which time it carried well into the twentieth.

The term "genius" is first encountered in Roman mythology where it was used to denote a procreative spirit allotted to every male at his birth.[1] The Roman "genius," in turn, has its roots in the Latin "gignere," meaning "to beget" or "sire."[2] In time this early conception was expanded to refer to a tutelary spirit that determined a man's character and fortunes as well as his total creative energies. It became a Roman custom to celebrate birthdays by offering sacrifices to one's

21

genius. Also, oaths taken in the name of one's genius were regarded as particularly sacred. A further expansion of the classical idea of genius led to the belief that every existing entity, such as a nation, city, legion, or even a house entrance, was under the protection of one of these spirits. In its most general sense, however, the Roman genius is the representation of a deity endowed with limited but superhuman powers. Similar to the gods, to whom these genii were subordinated, their influence was conceived as both beneficial and punitive in nature. In fact, it was frequently believed that every person was simultaneously attended by a protecting and a tormenting genius.[3]

A close parallel to the Roman genius exists in the Greek "demon." Like its Italian counterpart, the demon was conceived as a semideity, either good or evil, which presided over the destiny of a person, a tribe, a locality, and other discreet entities.[4] Quite different from this general view of the demon and the Roman genius is the one associated with Socrates and some of his contemporaries. It is this Socratic conception that closely resembles the modern idea of genius, in that the demon was regarded as a divine gift granted to select individuals only. According to this view, the poet, priest, philosopher, and sage communicated with the gods through the intervention of their demon. It is in this sense that Socrates called upon his demon and attributed most of his knowledge to intimations from it (Cahan, 1911:17-24). This conception of demons as the benevolent agents of the gods was generally endorsed by Plato[5] and found support in his doctrine of divine madness or "enthousiasmos."[6] In this view the poet is seen as divinely inspired, as an agent or servant of the gods who himself is devoid of talent. Inspiration and the gift of prophesy, however, were attainable only during particular states of mind, such as the loss of consciousness due to sleep or a mind affected by illness or "possession" (Rosen, 1969:83-84).

In spite of this association of inspiration with "enthousiasmos" or a kind of "mania," the Greek conception should not be equated with the modern idea of the mad genius. Contrary to frequent conjecture, the association of genius and madness is principally a development of the nineteenth century. Assertions that the classic notions of "demonic possession" and "enthusiasm" constitute proof of the alliance between genius and madness during antiquity appear to be oversimplifications. While Socrates, Plato, and others recognized the idea of divine "mania" or inspiration in relation to prophetic and poetic activity,[7] this divine disturbance was clearly distinguished from physical ailments and clinical insanity. Unlike the latter, the inspired madness of seers and poets was conceived as a virtue, a divine boon.[8] This position is celarly reflected in the *Phaedrus*:

> The greatest blessing come by way of madness, indeed of madness that is heaven sent. It was when they were mad that the prophetess at Delphi and the priestess at Dodona achieved so much for which both states and individuals in Greece are thankful: when sane they did little or nothing. As for the Sibyl and others who by the power of inspired prophesy have so often foretold the future to so many, and guided them aright, I need not dwell on what is obvious to everyone. [in Rosen:84]

Similarly, the Aristotelian assertion that extraordinary talent is characterized by a melancholic temperament does not mean, as is sometimes asserted, that Aristotle viewed insanity as the concomitant of genius. Insanity, according to Aristotle's reformulation of the Hippocratian humoral theory, did not occur in all melancholic individuals. Aristotle's melancholic man of distinction, observe the Wittkowers, is in possession of "a precarious gift, for if the black bile is not properly tempered (by yellow bile, phlegm, and blood), it may produce depression, epilepsy, palsy, lethargy, and what we would nowadays call anxiety complexes" (Wittkower and Wittkower, 1963:102). In short, while Aristotle argued that "all extraordinary men distinguished in philosophy, politics, poetry and the arts are evidently melancholic" (Wittkower and Wittkower, 1963:102), the "homo melancholicus," depending upon the particular balance of his "humors," could be either a man of distinction or a madman.

With the rise of Christianity the belief in spirits and semideities did not subside. In fact, the medieval period was an age of demonology in which the Greek demons and the Roman genii became transformed into a host of supernatural beings. Like their classical ancestors, the medieval ghosts, angels, goblins, saints, and witches all possessed the power to protect or torment mankind. But unlike the ancient times, the Middle Ages were not particularly fascinated by or even concerned with uncommonly endowed individuals. Not until the days of the Italian Renaissance was there renewed interest in those persons esteemed greatest in the arts and speculation. For these possessors of superior creative ability the term "genio" was reserved. However, "creativity" was thought of primarily in terms of an imitation of the established "masters" and of nature. Unlike the modern conception that stresses "originality" as the distinguishing feature of genius, the standard of the humanistic tradition was the "imitatio-ideal." It was not until about the mid-sixteenth century that this ideal was challenged by Leonardo, Vasari and Telesio, who insisted that the "genio" should not be just imitatively creative, but newly creative (Lange-Eichbaum, 1932:6). However, this attack on the "imitatio-ideal" did not become commonly accepted during the late Renaissance and, generally, had to be justified under the cloak of eclecticism and, particularly in the arts, by the dictum of faithfulness to nature (Zilsel, 1926:248-255).

As in the classical tradition, the unique attributes of the Renaissance "genio" commonly were described in terms of "melancholia" and "pazzia," or "madness."[9] But again, a distinction was maintained between the sane melancholics capable of rare accomplishments and those condemned to insanity. The Florentine Ficino, who popularized the Aristotelian idea of melancholy, regarded this type of temperament, in its application to distinguished men, as a divine gift that constituted a metonymy for Plato's divine "mania"—only the melancholic temperament was considered capable of creative enthusiasm. Hence, assessments of scholars and artists in terms of "pazzia" were generally not intended to convey the notion of insanity. "Pazzia" actually had numerous shades of meaning ranging from insanity to strangeness and eccentricity. Applied to great men, however, the term referred to qualities associated with the melancholic temperament, such as eccentricity, sensitivity, moodiness, and solitariness. These were far from negative qualities—emulating these manifestations of "melancholic behavior" was turned into a fad in sixteenth century Europe (Wittkower and Wittkower, 1963:98-105).

It is around the start of the eighteenth century that the term genius began to acquire its modern meaning, in the sense that it was used to denote a mysterious quality—a creative energy--that certain individuals were assessed as possessing. However, it was not until the middle of the eithteenth century that the name of genius became applied not just to the quality, but to the individuals manifesting this energy.[10] Defined as innate intellectual power with an extraordinary capacity for imaginative creation, original thought, invention, or discovery, genius was commonly distinguished from "talent" and mere educational prowess.[11] In this context, when the term was applied to individuals ("genii" or "geniuses"), it served to address those persons esteemed greatest in any department of art, speculation, or practice.

The eighteenth century marks a period in European history where the study of superior individuals, now called geniuses, attained unprecedented attention. Characterized by the German term "Genielehre," it was viewed as an exacting inquiry and a genuine contribution to the "science of human nature" (Fabian, 1966:XXVIII). While virtually all Enlightenment examinations of genius recognized certain subrational components, the leitmotif most frequently encountered stressed the rational processes of genius (Tonelli, 1973; Fabian, 1966).[12] Perhaps the model exposition of the Enlightenment conception of genius is Alexander Gerard's *An Essay On Genius*.[13] Defined as the faculty of invention "by means of which a man is qualified for making new discoveries in science, or for producing original works of art" (Gerard, 1774:8), genius was conceived as originating in an active imagination (Gerard:31). Asserting that an unbridled imagination constitutes a capricious and irresponsible faculty, he stipulated that it must be "subject to established laws" (Gerard:70). True genius, to Gerard, was only possible as a result of a synthesis or subtle interplay of four "powers": imagination, judgment, sense, and memory. "Mere imagination," he argued, "will not constitute genius. . . . As fancy (imagination) has an indirect dependence both on sense and memory, from which it received the first elements of all its conceptions, so when it exerts itself in the way of genius, it has an immediate connexion with judgment, which must constantly attend it, and correct and regulate its suggestions. This connexion is so intimate, that a man can scarce be said to have invented till he has exercised his judgment" (Gerard:36,37). Gerard was not along in viewing genius as an interplay of different mental "powers." To Duff, it was a balance of imagination, judgment, and taste;[14] Voltaire saw imagination in conjunction with memory and judgment; Kant, in a first version of his theory of genius (developed between 1770 and 1780), viewed it as a favorable proportion of sensibility, judgment, creative spirit, and taste; to Moses Mendelssohn, genius corresponded to a state of perfection of all mental powers working in harmony; to Shaftesbury, while he stressed the irrational traits of genius in terms of revelation and enthusiasm, a true genius did not infringe upon the rules of art—he needed knowledge and good sense (Tonelli, 1973).[15]

The prevailing Enlightenment conception of genius did, therefore, recognize certain "natural" or subrational components rooted primarily in the creative imagination. However, it pointedly established judgment, or reason, as a counterweight to these components and buttressed judgment with memory, taste, sense, sensibility, and so forth. Judgment was not only capable of averting "caprice" and "extravagance," but made madness a virtual impossibility for genius. As Gerard observed:

A perfect judgment is seldom bestowed by Nature, even on her most favored sons; but a very considerable degree of it always belongs to real genius. It may be remarked in the most incorrect and irregular artists; even when it has not force enough to discern every fault, or when the violence of imagination is too great to suffer it to be exerted with sufficient severity, yet still it prevents perfect absurdity, and restrains imagination from frantic excursions. Pindar is judicious even in his irregularities. The boldness of his fancy, if it had been under no control from reason, would have produced, not wild sublimity, but madness and frenzy. [Gerard:73-74]

The conception of the man of genius as "rational" not only constituted an Enlightenment ideal but, apparently, reflected the actual behavior of such men. Wittkower observes, for example, that even artists, known since antiquity for their propensity for "eccentric" behavior, complied with an image of the conforming artist. Since the Renaissance concept of the "melancholicus" had been supplanted by this newer image, "none of the great seventeenth-century masters—Rubens and Bernini, Rembrandt and Velasquez—was ever described as melancholic. . . . It was not until the romantic era . . . that melancholy appears once again as a condition of mental and emotional catharsis" (Wittkower, 1973:309).[16]

The late eighteenth and early nineteenth centuries, under the impact of the Romantic Movement, saw a profound change in the prevailing conception of genius.[17] Unlike the pre-Romantic analysis where genius for the arts and genius for science were assessed as being similarly constituted, Romantic thought dissociated the two, elevating the artist, and particularly the poet, to a position of preeminence[18] (Fabian: XXXI). Indeed, Kant, in a reformulation of his conception of genius (developed around 1800), confined the application of this term to artists only (see Hagen, 1877:652). While to Gerard's broader perspective all genius was rooted in "the faculty of *invention*; by means of which a man is qualified for making new discoveries in science, or for producing original works of art" (Gerard:8), the Romantics substituted "intuition," "phantasy," and "inspiration" as terms more suitable to

the supposed spontaneity of artistic genius (Wittkower, 1973:307).
Further, the earlier claim that imagination had to function under the
control of judgment or reason was discarded in favor of granting imagination clear predominance over judgment (Fabian:XL). Downgrading
reason was not designed to open the way for establishing a link between
genius and insanity, but to achieve freedom and independence for the
faculty seen as the vehicle for true genius–the aesthetic imagination
(Fabian:XIX; Morley in Young:XVI). Typical of this Romantic shift in
emphasis are the Schlegel brothers who, in their *Athenaeum*, insisted
that "The beginning of all poetry is to suspend the course and the laws
of rationally thinking reason, and to transport us again into the lovely
vagaries of fancy and the primitive chaos of human nature. . . . The free-
will of the poet submits to no law" (in Nordau, 1900:73).

The view of genius as a "law unto itself" is, of course, a reflection of
the prevailing mood of the times. The glowing optimism of the Ency-
clopedists, nourished by the ideas of rationalism, reason, and the laws
of consistency, had failed to generate a sustained support. This rationalistic view of the universe was supplanted by the Romantic "success"
formula, one that stressed the unconscious, the organic, the inherited
impulse, the individual "self,"–in short, all that was "natural." The
man of genius, reconstituted in the Romantic vision, became the embodiment of this new spirit and was enthusiastically hailed as the
"Erlösungskraft," or force of redemption, and the guiding light of the
age (Cahan, 1911:31). Underscoring this consecration of genius was a
sense of the inexplicable, the mystical. Whether conceived as the "force
of creation" (Lessing, Herder), a "natural endowment" (Kant), an instinct (Jean Paul, Schelling), intuition (Resevitz, Schopenhauer), or
naiveté (Schiller), the term genius suggested the mystical and the miraculous (Cahan, 1911:37). Reminiscent of Socratic and Platonic views,
the Romantics conceived of geniuses as the agents of a divine will, where
each in his own way proclaimed an essential "Urwahrheit" or primal
truth (Zilsel, 1918:8). "When Nature has work to be done," proclaimed
Emerson, "she creates genius to do it" (*Nature Addresses and Lectures*:
"The Method of Nature," 1895). Similarly, insisted Carlyle, genius constitutes "the most precious gift that Heaven can give to the earth . . . the
soul of a man actually sent down from the skies with a God's message
to us" (*Heroes and Hero-Worship*, II, 1840). Unlike the neoclassical in-
quiries into genius, which were rooted in the notion of an exacting
science of human nature ("Genielehre"), the Romantics' pronounce-

ments, as set forth by Coleridge, Shelly, and others, inevitably led to a kind of "Geniekult" or ecstatic celebration of genius. To Carlyle, the lessons of history were clear; the task of the masses was to engage in the veneration of genius. Indeed, he argued, "the heart of the whole business of the age . . . is to do it well" (in Zilsel, 1918:197).

The Romantic emphasis on "spontaneity," "intuition," and "creation," as well as the removal of the constraints of judgment, memory, taste, and knowledge, removed, as will be seen, an important obstacle to the association of genius and madness. Growing numbers began to echo Schopenhauer's pronouncement—based on a misinterpretation of Plato's fire of divine inspiration—that "genius is nearer to madness than the average intelligence" (Wittkower, 1973:308). The notion of the abnormality of genius had become so sufficiently popular by 1826 that Charles Lamb felt obligated to reassert the neoclassical view that genius "manifest itself in the admirable balance of all the faculties" ("The Sanity of True Genius":704). While genius was increasingly suspected as being somehow related to madness, this association was not firmly established during the Romantic period and lacked the "scientific" support of professional psychologists. In 1854, for example, a twenty-six page discussion of genius in the *Allgemeine Enzyklopädie Der Wissenschaften Und Künste* does not isolate madness as an attendant trait of genius; instead it notes that "the new psychology has determined, with considerable weight of consensus, that genius is characterized chiefly by originality, examplariness, totality, individuality, intuition, idealism and instinct . . . " (81).[19] As yet, no major shift from Enlightenment thinking is reflected.

It was not until the middle of the nineteenth century that psychological and pseudoclinical evidence was forthcoming and, thus, served to elevate the study of genius and madness to the rank of science. The French physician-psychiatrist Louis-François Lélut, who in 1836 wrote the first "pathography" or clinical history of genius (*Du Démon de Socrate*), scandalized the world of letters by declaring that Socrates was not figuratively, but literally the victim of hallucinations. Socrates' inclination "to take the inspirations of his conscience for the voice of a supernatural agent (his demon)," confirmed, in Lélut's opinion, that Socrates suffered from a "most undeniable form of madness" (Lélut, 1836:97-98).[20] Ten years later, in 1846, Lélut pronounced a similar judgment on Pascal (*L'Amulette De Pascal*). Following this line of inquiry, Jacques-Joseph Moreau, another French physician-psychiatrist, postulated in 1859 that genius was essentially a "névrose" or nervous affliction similar to idiocy. This assessment was based on a review of the clinical histories of some 180 persons of genius. In 1863, the famed Italian criminologist and physician-psychiatrist, Cesare Lombroso, while noting the numerous cases of sane geniuses, nevertheless endorsed Moreau's findings and concluded that genius was a degenerative psychosis of the epileptoid type (*Genio e follia*). In subsequent editions of this work, Lombroso adopted an even more one-sided stance and reduced his number of sane geniuses to six; even these, however, were discussed in terms of their "unperceived defects" (*The Man Of Genius*, 1891:353). In 1869, the English eugenicist Francis Galton formulated a hereditary theory of genius in which he postulated that all differences in human abilities, from the idiot to the great man, constitute deviations from the normal or average ability (*Hereditary Genius*). By the 1880's, with the publication of the fourth edition of Lombroso's *Genio e follia* and its subsequent translation into various languages, the topic of genius and madness had become a major theme of controversy in the Western world and, in particular, in France, Italy, Germany, England, and the United States. According to Lange-Eichbaum (1935), who provides the most comprehensive bibliography of the mad genius controversy, the monographs on this topic numbered well into the hundreds. Whereas a few—most notably Wilhelm Dilthey (1886), Bernard Shaw (1908), Sigmund Freud (1908, 1910), and Lewis Terman 1925, 1947)—argued against the association of madness and genius, the weight of publications were in the affirmative. Among those who endorsed the association were such authorities as Henry Maudsley (1886, 1908), Max Nordau (1900), Wilhelm Stekel (1909, 1917), Karl Jaspers (1926), Havelock Ellis (1927), and Ernst Kretschmer (1931). Indeed, at the turn of the twentieth century, the issue had generated enough interest to motivate Emile Zola, in the interest of science, to submit himself to an examination by fifteen psychiatrists (Trilling, 1950:163).

The stereotype of the mad genius reached an apex of popularity at the turn of the twentieth century (1880 to 1920). It has been largely discredited during the post-World War II period—at least in academic circles—and ceases to generate much contemporary interest. In fact, as Faris observes, the very concept of genius has virtually vanished from scholarly writings. This development, he argues, is quite possible due to "an aversion to popular usage, in which the term implies an exaggeration of the abilities and powers of men of achievement so that they appear to possess hereditary equipment of an order entirely apart from that of the rest of the population" (1968:457). Similar to Faris' position is Katz's observation that the study of charismatic imputation—such as genius—parallels the sociology of "deviance" (Katz, 1972:193). Accordingly, in both areas structural explanations have tended to supersede the earlier biological-determinist views. As such, in place of Galton's and Lombroso's emphasis on the hereditary nature of genius, the more recent focus is on the "sociological" causes and determinants of genius as exemplified by Faris (1940) and Lehman (1947). It is important to note that this change from a biological to a sociological focus has created the apparent need for new terminology. Many of the issues that traditionally have been associated with genius are now raised under headings such as creativity, ability, achievement motivation, intelligence, and intellect. Today, although there is a substantial body of literature that reflects continuing interest in individuals of extraordinary ability, this literature shies away from the term "genius," merely substituting such words as "intellect" and "intellectuals."[21] Even classifications of intellectual activity, such as Geiger's, in terms of "moral-evaluative," "cognitive-rational," and "symbolic-expressive" (Geiger, 1949), adhere rather closely to former classifications of genius in terms or genius for the arts, sciences, and so forth. Finally, Hofstadter's distinction between "intellect" and "intelligence" and his conception of intellect as the "critical, creative and contemplative side of mind" (1963:25) are closely related to the former insistence that the defining critierion of genius is not mere "talent" or "wit," but is rooted in originality, creation, and the power of imagination.

In conclusion, one can place the development of the concept of the mad genius firmly in the period between 1836 and 1950. The year 1836 can be seen as marking the opening of the dialogue with publication of Lélut's *Démon de Socrate*. The year 1950 has been chosen because it is determinable that the issue, since World War II, has no longer been of major concern. In antiquity and the Renaissance, the "homo melancholicus" who was a genius (or "distinguished man") was categorized quite apart from the "homo melancholicus" who was, because of an imbalance in his humors, insane. The prevailing attitude during the Enlightenment conceived of genius as a synthesis of different mental "powers." This interplay of agents—most commonly identified as imagination, judgment, sense, and memory—not only predisposed genius toward balance and rationality, but made madness a virtual impossibility. The Romantic view of genius, while it ceased to adhere to the notion of synthesis of "powers" and isolated imagination as the defining attribute, nevertheless stopped short of equating genius with clinical madness. It appears that the elimination of judgment, sense, and memory as "rational" counterweights to imagination was designed, primarily, not to underscore the notion of genius as irrational or diseased, but to provide a statement of independence from the constraints of tradition and authority. In more recent times (since World War II), the very idea of genius, with its attendant connotation of heredity as the primary formulative factor, has become distasteful to the holders of the ubiquitous idea that environment, not heredity, is primary. Therefore, our concern lies with the period from 1836 to approximately the midpoint of the twentieth century.

NOTES

1. A female counterpart was recognized, known as "juno."
2. It is suggested by Sprenger that the Latin "genius" was derived not from "gignere" but the Arabic "jinn," a collective name for a class of spirits (some good, some evil) that interfered in human affairs. However, this explanation is generally discounted by most authorities (see Lange-Eichbaum, 1935:28).
3. Two excellent sources describing the changing meanings of "genius" during antiquity are Jacob Cahan's *Zur Kritik des Geniebegriffs* (1911) and Edgar Zilsel's *Die Entstehung Des Geniebegriffes* (1926).
4. The notion of a demon as an exclusively evil spirit is apparently a late development that has its origin with the rise of Christianity (Cahan, 1911:17).
5. He viewed demons as the "beneficient averters of ill, [and] guardians of mortal men" (in N. Hirsch, 1931:277).
6. The idea of "enthousiasmos" was apparently not invented by Plato, but had its earliest spokesmen in Democritus and others (see Rosen, 1969:84).
7. Socrates distinguishes among four types of divine madness: prophetic, telestic, poetic, and erotic (see Rosen:84).
8. It should be noted that the "furor poeticus" and the "amabalis insania" of the Romans are in reference to the same phenomenon.
9. Vasari notes, for example, that Raphael was one of the few contemporary painters to be free of the commonly recognized eccentricities in painters (Zilsel, 1926:270).
10. The precise development of the term genius during the seventeenth and eighteenth centuries is elaborated in these excellent sources: Cahan (1911), Lange-Eichbaum (1935), Tonelli (1973), and Zilsel (1926).
It should be noted that in addition to the "modern" use of the term, during the seventeenth and eighteenth centuries the word genius was applied in at least two other contexts. Understood as a characteristic disposition, inclination, or

temper of mind, it was commonly applied not only to persons but also nations, eras, languages, institutions, and so on (i.e., the genius of the Catholic Church). Conceived in terms of natural ability or capacity, the term served to describe the special endowments suiting an individual to a particular line of work or interest (i.e., a genius for carpentry). While the term genius was used in various contexts (especially in the poetry of the times), as a scholarly concern the concept was limited exclusively to the manifestation of the highest form of innate creative ability.

11. As with almost anything, however, there are exceptions. Specifically, in Helvetius and Condorcet all mental differences among men are viewed not as innate but as the consequence of learning. This extremely rational view of genius, however, was not typical of the Enlightenment (see Lange-Eichbaum, 1929; also Ward, 1906).

12. Edward Young's *Conjectures On Original Composition* (1759), which constitutes perhaps the most noted exception to this rule (Tonelli, 1973:295), conceived of genius in terms more typical of the Romantic era. "An *Original*," Young argues, "may be said to be of a *vegetable* nature; it rises spontaneously from the vital roots of Genius; it *grows*, it is not *made*" (Young, 1918:12). Underscoring the essence of genius as being unconscious processes, he explains: "A *genius* differs from a *good understanding*, as a magician from a good architect; *that* raises his structure by means invisible; *this* by the skillful use of common tools. Hence genius has ever been supposed to partake of something divine" (Young, 1918:13). But unlike those assessments of genius that stress its more rational components—e.g., Sharpe, Duff, Beatie, Gerard, and others (see Fabian, 1966:IX-XLVIII)—Young's *Conjectures* is not so much an explanation of what defines genius and how it operates (Fabian, 1966:XIX) as it is a declaration of intellectual independence from the constraints of authorities and the conventional order (Fabian, 1966:XIX; Morley, 1918:XVI). It is quite possibly his emotional call for originality that accounts for Young's somewhat unorthodox treatment of genius (for the Enlightenment) and his particular popularity during the Romantic period.

13. Fabian notes that Gerard reflects most correctly the insights and convictions of the Enlightenment and his treatise has become the "sum and substance of what, about 1770, could be said on the vexing question on the nature of genius" (1966:XI). Wittkower, similarly, regards Gerard's contribution as preeminent (1973:306).

14. It should be noted that at this time imagination and fancy were generally used interchangeably, as were judgment and reason.

15. The idea that the real genius operates within limits and is not overwhelmed by "enthusiasm," "imagination," or "natural spontaneity" is also encountered in Dubos, André, Vauvenargues, Batteux, Dacier, Flögel, and Klopstock (Tonelli, 1973).

16. It is interesting to note that Diderot's *Rameau's Nephew*, an account of conversations with an eccentric musician, depicted as a shameless sensualist and immoralist, was not published during Diderot's lifetime. It was during the Romantic age that Goethe, recognizing in Rameau's nephew a prototype for the Romantic conception of genius, first presented it to the world (1805) in a German translation (see Barzun's Preface to *Rameau's Nephew And Other Essays*, 1964).

17. It is not suggested that the pre-Romantic period provided a monolithic conception of genius. Intellectual movements do not neatly follow at the heels of each other, but overlap and have their early spokesmen in preceding periods. Certainly, Young's contribution, while he wrote during the mid-eighteenth century, is more typically "Romantic" in tone. The attempt, here, is merely to describe changes in the dominant conception of genius.

18. In Germany, for example, the "Sturm und Drang" period of literature (roughly between 1770 and 1790) eventually became known as the "Geniezeit" or era of genius (*Der Grosse Brockhaus*: 161).

19. Translated by this author.

20. Translated by Anne McGovern.

21. While the concept of intellect can be said to constitute a more suitable substitute for genius, it appears that the notion of the intellectual, similar to genius, carries with it a number of unfavorable connotations. See Berger (1957), Brombert (1960) and Seeman (1958).

Positions on the Mad Genius Controversy

An Overview

> *The argument which you have produced is so learned and beautiful that it is impossible for him not to be mad and hypocondrically melancholic; and should he not be, he must become so for the sake of the beautiful things which you have said, and for the justness of the reasoning which you have produced.*

> [from Moliere's *Monsieur de Pourceaugnac*,
> Act 1, Sc.XI, trans. by Van Laun, 1880:109]

It is perhaps difficult for us now to understand how the issue of genius and madness could have been sustained, for a period of a hundred years, as a leading intellectual concern in the Western World. What provided a continued impetus to the controversy, however, was not the judgment of sanity or madness per se, but the specific arguments that produced these judgments. The tendency to produce relatively discrete arguments was especially pronounced among individuals who projected the image of the mad genius; they distinguished themselves one from another by stressing different determinants and varying degrees of pathology. This tendency provided a quality of richness to the mad genius literature and simultaneously infused an element of novelty that served to invite ensuing responses.

In this chapter, a breakdown of the various positions, with their attendant arguments, will be presented from the literature. An assessment of the distribution of these positions over time will follow. In addition, leading spokesmen for the particular positions will be identified, and certain patterns of professional affiliations will be noted.

Because it is impossible to locate and analyze the total body of literature relating to genius and the issue of madness, it becomes necessary, for this study, to reduce the universe of relevant data to manageable proportions. Such a procedure is justified providing no serious biases are introduced that preclude the forming of valid generalizations from the sample back to the universe. For purposes of this study, three works of reference have been chosen that provide a comprehensive and, reasonably nonselective, listing of relevant publications. These sources have served to locate materials published at different time periods during the genius controversy, which, it should be remembered, covers the approximate period from 1840 to 1950.

The primary source of reference consulted is the *British Museum Subject Index,* which contains the entries of books first published or reissued between 1880 and 1950 that have been added to the Library of the British Museum.[1] This source has proved ideally suited to this research, because it lists all acquired monographs that are classificable under the subject of "genius."[2] While the index fails to cross-reference journal articles or works on related subjects touching on genius, it does list the book acquisitions of a foremost library and, therefore, may be judged quite comprehensive in that area. For the period preceding 1880, two encyclopedic entries were consulted to provide a comparable list of sources. *The Encyclopaedia of the Social Sciences* (see Klinesberg, 1931) and *Der Grosse Brockhaus* (1930) provide comprehensive reviews of the mad genius exchange and, importantly, list the most relevant publications for the years 1837 to 1880. The *Encyclopaedia of the Social Sciences* is also distinguished by the fact that it lists numerous journal articles written on the topic of genius.

One additional specification is the limitation of the selection of materials to those sources appearing in English or German. This limitation seems not to introduce a serious bias, because most monographs on genius originally were written in either English or German or were translated into one of these. An exception to this rule, however, should be noted: while Lélut, Moreau, and Toulouse[3] apparently have not been translated into either language, their impact on the mad genius debate receives frequent acknowledgement. It was necessary, therefore, to examine their pertinent writings as well.

This selection procedure generated a list of 55 publications. Along with this central core of materials, this study includes additional materials of clear relevance to the problem, augmenting the list of materials to a total of 71 publications, of which 52 are books and 19 are journal articles. Because this sample contains eight individuals with two contributions, the number of authors whose works serve as the basis of this study is 63. Of this number, 54 writers specifically adopted a position on the mad genius controversy; the remaining nine wrote on other issues pertaining to genius. As can be seen, on the topic of genius, the issue of madness clearly provided a primary focus for scholarly discourse during the period under examination. The nine contributions that failed to address the madness issue have been analyzed, nonetheless, and are used in order to discern possible differences in the conception of genius when the focus is a topic other than madness.

The examination of these materials that treat genius in terms of the pathology question reveals the existence of ten more or less discrete positions or arguments on the issue, each discernible by its own underlying sense of logic. This does not imply mutual exclusivity of the positions, because in some instances a variety were employed simultaneously. A discussion of these basic arguments will help to underscore the complexity of the pathology question and serve as an aid in the subsequent analysis of this problem.

1. GENIUS AS DISEQUILIBRIUM

One explanation encountered throughout the period of the madness dialogue is the idea that genius constitutes a state of instability or disequilibrium in psycho-physical organization. This argument appears rooted in the still popular notion that an extraordinary natural endowment is generally coexistent with a compensating weakness. This view of compensation has found expression not only in attitudes toward the eccentric and the mad genius, but also in popular beliefs that regard the feebleminded as endowed with great physical strength, or conceive of unusually attractive individuals as being mentally deficient.[4] The judgment that genius involves a lack of equipoise was sustained by the assumption expressed by Royse (1891) and others that every individual is in possession of a finite amount of "nervous stimulus" or energy, which in the normal individual appears evenly apportioned among the various parts of the human organism. If, however, as in genius, "any one of these vital centers comes to arrogate to itself more than its normal share of nervous stimulus," argued Royse (184), "it is plain that one or more others must either suspend their natural functions or else diminish their activity." It is in this sense that the brain of the man of genius "tyrannizes over and practically annihilates one or more of the more purely material and animal centers of his mechanism" (Royse: 185). According to this view of disequilibrium, the debilitating consequences for genius are not always in the realm of mental health, but may result in a variety of afflictions pertaining to temperament, morality, or the physical order. The often encountered assertion that genius is a frequent victim of "moral insanity" appears to have its origins, in part, in the notion of the unstable equilibrium. When applied to the state of mental health, the genius becomes viewed as a one-sided eccentric whose ill-balanced mental structure is the result of a disproportionate growth of a single mental faculty (e.g., Maudsley, 1908:67).

2. GENIUS AS DEGENERACY

Perhaps the most controversial indictment of genius is contained in the degeneracy argument, encountered most often in the second half of the nineteenth and early twentieth century. This concept, first formulated by Morel around 1850 and popularized by Lombroso, Nordau, and others,[5] conceived of degeneracy as a state of biological inferiority caused by a reversion to an earlier type, or a change from a "higher" to a less complex organism. This state of "morbid deviation from an original type" is biologically transmissible, argued Morel, so that the "mental progress already checked in his own person (the degenerate's), finds itself menaced also in his descendents" (in Nordau, 1900:16). Adding to the controversy of the degeneracy argument was the assertion that the person of genius is derived from the same pathological stock as the criminal, the prostitute, the anarchist, and the pronounced lunatic (Nordau, 1900:vii). For the born victim of degeneracy, Babcock offered little consolation, recognizing four imposed alternatives, each marked by accompanying perils:

First, and most prominent in the order of frequency is an early death. Second, he may swell the criminal ranks. Third, he may become mentally deranged and ultimately find his way into a hospital for the insane. Fourth, and least frequently, he startles the world by an invention or discovery in science or by an original

composition of great merit in art, music or literature. He is then
styled a genius. [1895:752]

Underscoring the membership of genius in the same "anthropological
family" with criminals and lunatics was the assertion that all degenerates display the same mental and somatic characteristics. To Nordau,
the physical "stigmata" most frequently encountered in all types of
degeneracy are such factors as an asymetrical face or cranium, stunted
growth, protruding ears, squint-eyes, harelips, irregularities in the form
and position of the teeth, and webbed or supernumerary fingers (1900:
17). The nonphysical "brand-marks" of degeneracy Nordau identified
as the decrease in the sense of morality ("moral insanity"), an un-
bounded egoism ("ego-mania"), impulsiveness, excessive emotionalism,
pessimism, a disinclination to action of any kind, and a preoccupation
with mystical and religious questions (Nordau:18-22).

While the "higher degenerate," or man of genius, shares these characteristics with the "lower degenerates," the genius, in turn, was said
to display signs of degeneration peculiar to his type. Lombroso recognized nearly thirty of these, including such characteristics as smallness
of body, pallor, emaciation, stammering, precocity, somnambulism,
sterility, originality, and left-handedness (1891:6-37). While the biological aberrations of all degenerates were believed to result in a shared
susceptivity to emotional instability, hypersensitiveness and a marked
liability to psychoses, neuroses and numerous psychopathic complaints;
it was generally maintained by Lombroso, Babcock, and others that the
mental state of genius constitutes an affliction distinct from those of
the other degenerates. "We may confidently affirm," claimed Lombroso, "that genius is a true degenerative psychosis belonging to the
group of moral insanity, and may temporarily spring out of other
psychoses, assuming their forms, though keeping its own special peculiarities, which distinguish it from all others" (1891:333).

Influenced by notions of evolutionary theory, the degeneracy model
stipulated that the atavistic genius was incapable of perpetuating its
kind. "Genius cannot beget genius" was a commonly voiced dictum.
All the "higher degenerate" is capable of, argued Nordau, is to trans-
mit to its "offspring, in a continuously increasing degree, its peculiarities . . . malformations and infirmities" (1900:16). Fortunately, he
observed, the degenerate is "soon rendered sterile, and after a few
generations often dies out before it reaches the lowest grade of organic degradation" (Nordau:16). Given the premise of the hereditary

nature of degeneracy, Maudsley proclaimed boldly, "It is no exaggeration to say that there is hardly ever a man of genius who has not insanity or nervous disorder of some form in his family" (1886:655).

3. GENIUS AS DIFFERENTIATED FROM THE TOTALLY PATHOLOGICAL "QUASI-GENIUS"

A variation of the degeneracy model is provided by those who maintained a distinction between the sane men of genius and a group generally identified as "quasi-genii" or "pseudo-great men." In the classic degeneracy statements (i.e., Lombroso, Nordau, Babcock), the sane man of genius appears as a blessing of the past; most, if not all, contemporary "greats" were viewed as the unfortunate products of the ongoing process of degeneration. In the retrenchment of this position (most notably W. Hirsch, 1897; Schwarz, 1916), the expressed emphasis is on the continued sanity of "true" genius, with the taints of degeneracy confined to numerous aspiring "near-greats." With regard to the latter, Hirsch observed:

> In those partially gifted degenerates, those pseudo-geniuses, certain typical characteristics are hardly ever wanting. In childhood they already show that vanity and self-sufficient arrogance, that foolhardy conceit which never leave them through life. [135]

> [They] love to wallow round in sloughs and puddles, to sweep forward what is dirty and vulgar, and to amuse themselves with such things. This preference may in many cases be accounted for by such a perversion of the feelings and by a mental degeneracy. Other abnormal impulses, especially of a sexual origin, appear in the works of degenerates. [137]

The aspiring "near-greats" most susceptible to the charge of degeneracy were generally those innovative individuals who transgressed certain artistic or intellectual conventions. To Hirsch, the literary and artistic works of the modern Realists and Naturalists most fully displayed the "pestilential" malady of degeneration (216-217).

But while, in accordance with this model, the label of degeneracy is reserved for only certain "quasi-genii," all men of genius are defined as especially vulnerable to various mental afflications. To Schwarz, while the "true" genius is essentially sane, he is nevertheless susceptible to "psychical degeneration," a condition defined as an "inherited feeble resistency to mental strains caused by intellectual pregnancy" (389).

4. GENIUS AS A NEURASTHENIC CONDITION PRODUCED BY OVERWORK

The claim that genius is frequently subject to neurotic conditions produced by the strains of mental exertion received the greatest attention in those assessments that viewed genius as essentially sane or mildly afflicted.[6] Typical of this position is Ellis' examination in 1927 of one thousand British persons of genius. Conceding only a slightly greater liability to insanity among men of genius (computed at 4.5 percent) compared to the general population (estimated at between 1 and 2 percent), Ellis rejected all views of genius and insanity as concomitant. As if by way of concession, however, he argued that unlike the improbability of grave mental disorders, "nervous symptoms of vaguer and more atypical character" are commonly encountered in geniuses (Ellis: 177). These lesser "irritable conditions of the nervous system" were seen principally as the consequence of mental exhaustion as well as the results of impoverishment, rejection, persecution, and various other social determinants. According to this view of the neurasthenic genius, the principal sources of suffering are said to inhere in the act of original creation. "In creative activity," observed Tsanoff, "genius is at the ultimate limit of tension, the utmost of reach, of intensity, penetration. Human nature here unfolds the plentitude of its powers; but it also commits itself utterly and makes overwhelming demands on itself" (1949:29). In this view, only few geniuses are judged capable of escaping all nervous disorders, for it is in the nature of the genius to engage his intellectual powers "recklessly" to their utmost limits of intensity.

5. GENIUS AS PRODUCT OF PATHOLOGICAL STATE PRODUCED BY GENETIC CONFLICT OR OUTSIDE AGENTS

In this view of genius, popular in the 1920s and thereafter, suffering and psychic conflict are seen as requisites to creative production. Specifically, outside agents such as drugs, intoxicants, and gradually debilitating ailments—or genetic frictions produced by hybridization—are judged to constitute a crucial part in the making of genius. The psychic tensions produced by such elements are seen as fostering a reduction or near-paralysis in the inhibitory mechanisms and, in this way, allowing the previously restrained creative powers to become unleashed.[7] The ideas of Jacobson (1926) afford an excellent example of this view of genius. Arguing on behalf of the dual nature of personality, he stipulated that all latent creative powers reside in a "secondary self." Whereas in most men the socially conscious "primary self" is seen as successfully stifling the "secondary self," genius always involves the temporary domination of the "secondary self." Because the societal tendency to censor or smother self-expression is very strong, insisted Jacobson, it becomes virtually impossible for the "primary self" to be even temporarily usurped. Such usurption, nearly impossible in healthy individuals, is made possible as a result of certain pathological states. "The release of creative secondary personalities," to Jacobson, "would seem to depend upon some sort of intoxication, with resulting paralysis of inhibitions. This is obviously true of alcohol, as well as of the toxins of tuberculosis" (Jacobson: 6).[8]

A related explanation of this type of argument is provided by Kretschmer (1931), where hybridization of peoples is viewed as a kind of "Fermentunruhe" or unsettling precondition for genius. The hybrid individual, subject to constant tensions by his inherent "germinal hostility," is most likely to develop that complicated character type called genius. It is the nature of the character of "warring heredities," argued Kretschmer, that "produces the unstable equilibrium, the emotional exuberance, and the restless inner drive which lifts genius high above the peaceful exercise of traditional occupations and forbids it satisfaction with the ordinary pleasures of life" (Kretschmer: 67).

6. GENIUS AS PATHOLOGICAL BY VIRTUE OF THE SELECTIVE GRANTING OF FAME

For the period under review, the prevailing conception was of genius as a nearly constant quality, markedly obvious and unable to escape detection for very long. Those endowed with this rare gift were seen as destined to rise above all conceivable obstacles and impose, inevitably, their stamp upon mankind.[9] The rejection of this assumption in the writings of Jaspers (1926) and Lange-Eichbaum (1932, 1935) serves as a basis for yet another position on the issue of madness. To both men, genius was seen essentially as a social label assigned selectively to particular men of talent but not to others. While to Lange-Eichbaum, a "Hochtalent," or individual with exceptional talent, is seen as possessing one key attribute facilitating labeling, the imputation of genius required generally one additional ingredient—some element of pathology. In this view, the presence of "bionegative" attributes[10] promotes the attainment of fame in two ways. It served to heighten susceptibility to dreams and phantasies stimulating achievement and creativity and, most importantly, sets the individual apart, in a dramatic way, from all average men. To Lange-Eichbaum, it is the element of pathology in the man of talent that allows others to regard him in terms of the mysterious and divine; it is this that suggests a magical quality to the creative process and imbues the individual with a sense of self-sacrifice and the tragic. "This does not signify that genius is itself 'insane'," observed Lange-Eichbaum, "but that the mentally disordered person is more likely than the sane person to become famous, and that the fame of the mentally disordered person more often than the fame of the mentally healthy person leads to elevation to the rank of genius" (1932:140). It is in this sense, observed Lange-Eichbaum, that "nine-tenths of genius is ultimately associated with 'insanity,' with psychopathy or psychosis" (1932:142).

Jaspers' position differs from Lange-Eichbaum's in one important respect. Although he believed the term genius to be a socially assigned label generally granted to "sick" men of talent, he did not feel that this tendency applies to all historical times. What distinguished the nineteenth and twentieth centuries from the eighteenth, for example, is a general mood or inclination that craved the mysterious, the unusual, the primitive, the distant, the undefinable, and the blatantly diseased.[11] While the Enlightenment rewarded healthy and rational individuals with the distinction of genius, argued Jaspers, modern times have shown a preference for those men of talent who are clearly diseased and, specifically, schizophrenic (1926:148-149). To Lange-Eichbaum, then, those elevated to the rank of genius were nearly always mentally disordered, whereas to Jaspers this applied only to certain periods in history and, in particular, to modern times.[12]

7. GENIUS AS CRIMINALLY DISPOSED

The degeneracy argument was first to provide a "scientific" explanation linking geniuses to criminals as members of the same "anthropological" family. To Maudsley, Lombroso, and others, the "higher degenerates" were seen as incapable of adapting to existing circumstances, a condition of "morbid variation" certain to lead to extinction. But while the conception of the "higher degenerate" with distinctly recognizable physical and mental "stigmata" began to lose popularity during the latter part of the madness controversy, an offshoot of the degeneracy model developed that stressed the nature of genius as being uniquely criminal, rather than merely nonconformist or mentally diseased. The issue of madness was relegated to lesser importance, and the emphasis became centered on the question of criminality and social control. To Rhodes, a spokesman for this argument, the psychology of genius is seen as a "sublime hatred" for all existing social arrangements, bent on their destruction. Borrowing from Freudian terminology, he saw the man of genius as differing from the "normal" man—due to some innate deficiency—by his failure to capitulate to the "reality principle of society." Comparing the genius to the criminal, he recognized the same imperfect adjustment to society "since genius strives either in action to overthrow the existing order and introduce another in harmony with it, or, in thought and imagination, to construct a new world. In either case there is a clash between the aims of genius and the existing reality principle for which society stands" (Rhodes, 1932:272). Given the definition of genius as criminal, the advocacy of control and regulation appeared only logical. Hyslop, particularly concerned with the danger of the "great irresponsibles," went so far as to draft a proposal to Britain's Royal Commission on Lunacy and Mental Disorder in which he sought the confinement of all "subversivists" and the "morally perverted" judged harmful to the community (1925:276). Similarly, he contended that Britain "should deny itself the thankless task of offering itself as an 'asylum' for alien perverts and subversivists. Certain it is that England has been in danger of becoming the dumping ground, or 'Asylum of the World,' owing to the misguided hospitality it has extended hitherto to alien degenerates, irresponsibles, and undesirables" (1925:281).

8. GENIUS AS SUBLIMATION AND SUBSTITUTE GRATIFICATION

According to this view, genius cannot be regarded as degeneracy or psychosis; rather, it has its origin in the fixation of infantile desires, which, if sublimated, issue forth in acts of imaginative creation.[13] These acts are conceived as substitutes for infantile fantasies, and primarily as the transformed products of a pronounced sexual libido. Indeed, what distinguishes the man of genius, in this view, is the possession of a "surplus" libido that resists adaptation to societal demands. Unlike the criminal and pervert who surrenders to the dictates of his libido, the genius is seen as rechanneling his libidinal energies and thus, at least outwardly, making an adequate adaptation to societal expectations.

Those writers identified with the theory of sublimation—in my sample, most notably Freud and Stekel—differed in their views on whether sublimation led to emotional stress and mental disorder. To Freud (1910), the utilization of libidinal energies on behalf of higher intellectual and aesthetic concerns allows the genius to escape the fate of neurosis; it is the failure to successfully sublimate fixated infantile desires that creates a nearly insurmountable disposition to "obsessional neurosis." To Stekel, in comparison, the struggle inherent in the sublimation of libidinal impulses is seen to lead to an inevitable disposition to neurosis; as such, all men of genius are judged neurotic. Indeed, he argued, the neurotic condition constitutes the germ of creation and the source of all progress. While every person is seen in terms of at least a "latent" neurosis, the genius, due to his extraordinary degree of libidinal vigor, is clearly neurotic (1909:8).

9. GENIUS AS MENTALLY SANE

Central to this argument is the assertion that genius, far from disequilibrium, constitutes a state of perfect harmony of all mental faculties.[14] It is the fortunate arrangement of these faculties that, in this view, permits their best utilization and warrants the assessment of genius as healthy and constituting the "complete human," singularly capable of the rarest intellectual feats. Consistent with this assertion is the claim that all intellectual processes in genius are subject to the same basic "psychological laws" encountered in average men. In those instances where superior minds are recognized as mentally afflicted, the abnormal condition is said to play at best a minor part in fostering creativity; genius creates in spite of and not because of infirmities.

10. GENIUS AS ABOVE AVERAGE IN TERMS OF MENTAL AND PHYSICAL HEALTH

The traditional picture of the man of genius as suffering from numerous mental and physical anomalies received a particularly strong challenge from a number of statements based on findings from clinical examinations of so-called "gifted children." These youthful individuals were defined as geniuses by their examiners based on their high performances on intelligence tests. Most famous of these studies are those of Hollingworth (1926), Carroll (1940) and, in particular, the five-volume *Genetic Studies of Genius* conducted by Terman (1925), Cox (1926), Burks (1930), Oden (1947; see Terman) and others.[15] In place of the prevailing, traditional view of the genius as an undersized, weak neurotic with a large head, these investigators all concluded that their sample populations were overwhelmingly comprised of subjects who were not only normal but, in fact, excelled in terms of physical and mental health. In the words of Burks, "the typical gifted child was found to suffer from fewer headaches, to exhibit fewer symptoms of 'general weakness' or of 'nervousness,' to mature earlier, to display more physical energy, and to be better nourished, taller, and heavier than the average child" (1930:209). With regard to the subjects' head size, Hollingworth noted that "the gifted have . . . larger heads than the ungifted, but only in accordance with their greater size in other respects" (in Carroll, 1940:71). Commenting on the frequency of neurotic disorders, Carroll concluded that "although individuals with any degree of intelligence may become involved in neurotic difficulties, the tendency is much greater in the cases of humble intelligence" (Carroll: 88). Oden and Terman, in their follow up study spanning twenty-five years, noting the large proportion of gifted subjects who managed to improve or entirely recover from all types of mental disturbances, proposed that superior intelligence may, indeed, be responsible for the actual correction of maladjustments (1947:123).

INTERPRETATION

In reviewing these basic arguments it becomes apparent that some degree of pathology or aberration is central to eight, with the emphasis on behalf of sanity confined to two. Each of these positions is distinguished by a unique sense of logic that highlights their differences rather than existing commonalities. In order to focus on what is central to this study of the genius controversy—the question of madness—it becomes necessary to collapse these arguments into two general camps: those arguing for and those arguing against pathology. Such a decision permits an overall assessment of the distribution of the pro and con judgments over time.

The polemical nature of the genius controversy presents certain difficulties for the two-fold classification of the individual monographs. Occasionally, the author's basic position on the issue—whether the association of genius and madness is rejected or endorsed—is subject to possible differences in interpretation. It has been found that an author's explicit rejection of this association cannot always be taken at face value. Quite frequently, all that was intended by such a rejection was to discredit a particular position on the issue. While many attacked Lombroso's formulation of the problem,[16] for instance, few chose to redefine genius as healthy or sane. Instead, genius became merely recast as a victim of some lesser affliction, where the degree of pathology changed from psychosis or degeneracy to neurosis, an unstable equilibrium, or some other malady.

Because it has proved impossible, therefore, to always accept the author's explicit statement on the issue, it has been decided to employ the ten basic arguments for the dychotomization of the individual monographs. Accordingly, whenever an author is found to endorse at least one of the positions, previously numbered in this chapter as 1 through 7,[17] he is classified as supporting the association of genius and pathology; similarly, the support for position No. 9 or No. 10 leads to the classification of genius as healthy. The decision to subsume arguments No. 3 and No. 7 under the pathology position requires justification. While No. 3 (genius as differentiated from the totally pathological "quasi-genius") reserved the judgment of degeneracy for only those "near-greats" who transgressed certain artistic or intellectual conventions, the entire range of genius was seen, nevertheless, as particularly susceptible to a variety of mental afflictions. Similarly, argument No. 7 (genius as criminally disposed) proceeded from the assumption that not just the criminally disposed, but all men of genius—by virtue of some innate deficiency—are generally incapable of submitting to the dictates of society.

One final specification pertains to argument No. 8 (genius as sublimation and substitute gratification). It should be recalled that the major spokesmen for this position, Freud and Stekel, differed on whether sublimation could lead to stress and mental disturbances. It was therefore necessary to place these individuals into appropriately different categories. Freud belongs with the "con" position evidenced by No. 9 and No. 10; Stekel joins the "pro" group.

The application of this procedure has led to the following breakdown in the sample population of 54 who expressed a position on the pathology question: for the total period under review, from 1836 till 1950, 39 were found to describe genius in terms of at least one of the pathology arguments; the remaining 15 defined genius as healthy and sane. The overall pathology: health ratio is, therefore, 2.6:1. The division of this 114 years' period into three nearly equal time spans (1836 to 1879; 1880 to 1919; 1920 to 1950) reveals a gradual decrease in the popularity of the pathology position. For the opening period of the genius dialogue (1836 to 1879), the pathology position enjoys a nearly unanimous consensus for a ratio of 7:1, where the lone dissenter is an anonymous writer of a journal article.[18] For the time span 1880 to 1919 the disparity in arguments becomes gradually narrowed to a count of 19 to 7 or a 2.7:1 ratio. The period after 1920 marks a further reduction in the pathology: health ratio to 1.9:1 with its distribution of 13 to 7 (see Table 3.1).

The near unanimity on behalf of the pathology stance during the years 1836 to 1879 deserves to be seen as the opening phase of the madness dialogue, when the first "scientific" statements appear proclaiming the medical association of genius with madness. Reactions to the pronouncements of Moreau, Lombroso, and others follow during subsequent years (the period from 1880 to 1919) and take the form, primarily, of qualified endorsements of these earlier positions. After 1920, a clear majority of monographs continues to reflect pro-pathology sentiments; increasingly, however, the emphasis shifts to the recognition of "milder" forms of pathology and, in a few instances, the image of the mentally and physically superior man of genius is established. In spite of the gradual mitigation in the frequency and intensity of the pro-pathology verdicts, the overriding impression of the madness controversy, for its entire duration, is that the view of the aberrant genius remains dominant. This judgment is supported by the pathology: health ratios as well as the large number of the different pathology arguments (No. 1 through No. 7) developed to support this association.

A question naturally follows: who then were the people to promote the image of the mad genius? An examination of standard biographical reference materials reveals, most strikingly, that a majority of participants in the genius controversy were members of the medical professions.[19] Information indicating professional affiliation has been located for 46 of those 54 individuals who addressed the issue of genius and pathology. Of the 46 people for whom information is available, 26 earned a medical degree and are generally classifiable under the category

TABLE 3.1
Position on Issue

Genius as Pathology	Genius as Healthy
1836-1879	
(1836; 1846) Lélut, Louis-Francois	(1861) Anonymous
(1859) Moreau, Jacques-Joseph	
(1859) Noack, Ludwig	
(1863) Lombroso, Cesare (1891)	
(1863) Schilling, Johann A. (1866)	
(1869) Galton, Francis (1892)	
(1877) Hagen, Friedrich W.	
1880-1919	
(1884) Radestock, Paul	(1886) Dilthey, Wilhelm
(1885) Sully, James	(1887) Stevenson, William G.
((1886; 1908) Maudsley, Henry	(1895) Shaw, Bernard G. (1908)
(1886) Sanborn, Kate	(1896) Toulouse, Édouard
(1891) Royse, N. K.	(1902) Padovan, Adolfo
(1891) Nisbet, J. F. (1912)	(1908; 1910) Freud, Sigmund (1958; 1957)
(1892) MacDonald, Arthur	(1909) Hoesch-Ernst, Lucy
(1892) Nordau, Max (1900)	
(1895) Babcock, Warren L.	
(1895) Auerbach, A.	
(1896) Türck, Hermann (1914)	
(1897) Hirsch, William	
(1901; 1909) Möbius, Paul J.	
(1904) Ellis, Havelock (1927)	
(1909) Hoffmann, Richard A.	
(1909; 1917) Stekel, Wilhelm	
(1910) Sadger, J.	
(1914) Armstrong-Jones, Robert	
(1916) Schwarz, Osias L.	
1920-1950	
(1923) Hinkle, Beatrice M.	(1920; 1949) Hock, Alfred
(1925) Hyslop, Theo. B.	(1925) Terman, Lewis M. (1959)
(1925) Marks, Jeannette (1926)	(1926) Hollingworth, Leta S.
(1926) Jacobson, Arthur C.	(1926) Cox, Catharine M. (1959)
(1926) Jaspers, Karl	(1930) Burks, Barbara S. (1961)
(1927; 1930) Lange-Eichbaum,	(1940) Carroll, Herbert A.
Wilhelm (1935; 1932)	(1947) Oden, Melita H. and
(1931) Hirsch, Nathaniel D.	Terman, L. M. (1959)
(1931) Kretschmer, Ernst	
(1932) Rhodes, Henry T.	
(1939) Baisch, Helga	
(1940) Moorman, Lewis J.	
(1947) Bowerman, Walter G.	
(1949) Tsanoff, Radaslav A.	

Note: The dates preceding the names indicate the years when monographs were first published. In those instances where a later edition was examined, the dates following the names indicate the years of publication.

of "physician-psychiatrist." Of the 26 people with a medical degree, all but four promoted at least one of the basic pathology arguments. Importantly, for those remaining 20 individuals who are not members of the medical profession, the pathology: health ratio was found to be nearly 1:1, with a frequency count of 11:9 (see Table 3.2).

Professional background information also has been gathered for six of those nine individuals who wrote on genius but failed to take issue on the question of madness. Only one of these is found to be a member of the medical profession.

One final observation pertains to six individuals who have been classified as psychologists. These are distinguished by the fact that they all endorsed a pro-health argument and, more specifically, promulgated the idea that physical and emotional superiority were associated with genius. It should be noted that five of these six psychologists based this judgment on their examinations of "gifted" children, or "young" men of genius (see Table 3.3).

In conclusion, the image of the pathological genius—the dominant view throughout the period of the madness controversy—was fostered primarily by "physician-psychiatrists." Those medical men who chose to write on genius did so almost entirely in the context of genius and madness, with the pronounced verdict on behalf of pathology. Of those individuals who challenged the dominant view of genius, a majority were members of the other, nonmedical disciplines, with a large proportion of professional psychologists.

TABLE 3.2
Position on Issue by Medical vs. Nonmedical Affiliation

Position on Issue	Affiliation		
	Authors with Medical Degrees	Authors with No Medical Degrees	
Genius as Pathology	22	11	33
Genius as Healthy	4	9	13
	26	20	46

TABLE 3.3
Authors with Degrees in Medicine* or Psychology**
(for 46 out of 54 individuals who address issue)

Genius as Pathology	Genius as Healthy
1836-1879	
Lélut*	
Moreau*	
Noack	
Lombroso*	
Galton*	
Hagen*	
1880-1919	
Sully	Dilthey
Maudsley*	Stevenson*
Sanborn	Shaw
Nisbet	Toulouse*
Babcock*	Freud*
Nordau*	Hoesch-Ernst
Auerbach*	
Türck	
Hirsch, W.*	
Möbius*	
Ellis*	
Hoffmann	
Stekel*	
Sadger*	
Armstrong-Jones*	
Schwarz	
1920-1950	
Hinkle*	Hock*
Hyslop*	Terman**
Marks	Hollingworth**
Jacobson*	Cox**
Jaspers*	Burks**
Lange-Eichbaum*	Carroll**
Kretschmer*	Oden**
Rhodes	
Moorman*	
Bowerman	
Tsanoff	

(for 6 of 9 individuals who did not address issue)

Walshe, Walter*
Cooley, Charles H.
Constable, Frank C.
Ward, Lester
Kárpáth, Ludwig
Koller, Armin

NOTES

1. A subject index is not provided by the Library of Congress for the period prior to 1950.

2. Those indices covering the period since 1925 pose a minor problem due to the practice of listing entries under the combined heading of "genius: intelligence: ability." Quite clearly, many of the sources listed under this triple heading address a variety of issues ranging from the measurement of intelligence to discussions of mathematical ability. It became necessary, therefore, to exclude those sources that did not deal specifically with the category of men of genius. Consequently, the procedure adopted was to select only those entries that contained in the title the term "genius" or made specific reference to distinguished individuals.

3. Toulouse wrote a famous account based on his physical and mental examination of Zola.

4. With regard to genius, Babcock observes, for example: "Undoubtedly, the preponderance of great natural gifts of mind . . . entails a corresponding deficiency in other parts of the mental and physical economy, and though in many respects the man of genius may well be the subject of envy, he may in other regards, as consistently be the object of pity" (1895:750). Similar pronouncements are encountered in the writings of Armstrong-Jones (1914), Lélut (1846), Maudsley (1908), Möbius (1902), Moreau (1859), Royse (1891), Sully (1885), and many others.

5. Statements typical of the degeneracy position also are to be found in Baisch (1939), MacDonald (1892), Nisbet (1891), and Radestock (1884).

6. See especially Bowerman (1947), Ellis (1927), Royse (1891) and Tsanoff (1949).

7. This view finds clearest enunciation in Baisch (1939), Jacobson (1926), Kretschmer (1931), Marks (1926), and Moorman (1940). A variation on this type of argument is encountered in Edmund Wilson's *The Wound and the Bow* (not part of sample), where genius is viewed as a manifestation of successful or nearly successful compensation for perceived psychic inferiority. This sense of inferiority is seen often as physical in its genesis and finds exemplication in Wilson's interpretation of the Demosthenes legend (1941).

8. In an editorial to the *Medical Times,* Jacobson, lamenting the decline in the quality of American literature, offered the following observation: "We believe that there is another aspect to this matter—a medical reason why the candles are snuffed; why the fires smolder; why genius is dead; why the descending curtain signalizes the end of the show. The decline in tuberculosis coincides with the decline in creative writing. . . . In the healthful days to come we may not apprehend the past role of tuberculosis in quickening creative faculties; and by way of compensation for good health we may lack certain cultural joys" (in Moorman, 1940: XV). With regard to the prohibition of alcohol, Jacobson offered an equally mixed evaluation. Like tuberculosis, alcohol has its bad side, but without it, "Poe . . . would be pallid stuff" (Jacobson, 1926:38).

9. This argument constitutes a major conclusion of Galton's classic study on the hereditary nature of genius (1869).

10. The term "bionegative" is favored by Lange-Eichbaum over terms such as "illness," "insanity," and "madness," because he believed it to be value-neutral and, therefore, of greater scientific use.

11. This observation receives support from Mario Praz, especially as it applies to the Romantic era (see *The Romantic Agony*, 1951).

12. As Ned Polsky correctly observed, Lange-Eichbaum may clearly be regarded as a forerunner of the labeling perspective current in sociology (1971: 193). The same is doubtlessly true for Jaspers. But even though both men viewed genius not as a biological reality but as a socially assigned label, they failed to extend this framework to the issue of mental illness. To both, mental disease was a concrete medical reality, and not subject to social contingencies of labeling. It should be remembered that the labeling perspective, when applied to this concern, makes no such assumption, but adopts what has previously been called an "agnostic" stance.

13. This argument finds its clearest formulation in Freud (1908, 1910), Hinkle (1923), and Stekel (1909, 1917).

14. Typical of this position are an anonymous statement (1861), Dilthey (1886), Hock (1949), Padovan (1902), Shaw (1895), Stevenson (1887), and Toulouse (1896).

15. Volume five of the *Genetic Studies* is not part of this examination because it was published after 1950, the date chosen as the approximate termination of the mad genius controversy.

16. For an annotated bibliographical listing of those who specifically endorsed or rejected Lombroso's statement of the problem, see Lange-Eichbaum, 1932:49-54.

17. It should be remembered that those who projected the image of the mad genius, while they generally emphasized one particular model, occasionally endorsed other pathology arguments as well.

18. See "Reason, Genius, And Madness," *Medical Critic And Psychological Journal*, 1861, pp. 132-142. This does not mean that other statements do not exist for this period that argued against the association of genius and madness. It must be remembered that the sample selection procedure for this study, with four exceptions, precluded the examination of monographs not published in English or German. As such, a known French statement on behalf of sanity written by P. Flourens (*De la raison du genie et de la folie*, Garnier, Paris, 1861) did not become part of this study. Underscoring the scarcity of the pro-sanity argument during this early period is the fact that the anonymous English statement relies almost exclusively on Flourens for support of its position.

19. No single source of reference contained biographical accounts for all of these. Therefore, a variety of standard reference materials had to be consulted, ranging from the "national biographies (i.e., *The National Cyclopaedia of American Biography; Allgemeine Deutsche Biographie*) to the more condensed works providing only demographic data (i.e., *Who Was Who; Wer Ist Wer*).

Implications for Labeling in Two Conceptions of Genius

The Romantic and the Rational

Responsibility for the nineteenth century change in the prevailing conception of genius from sane to mad cannot rest entirely with "bourgeois" or "philistine" labelers. The men of genius, particularly the Romantics, share considerable "blame" for this redefinition. They often underscored by word and action that the artist, and by extension all men of genius, is a member of a touchy tribe—"genus irritabile." They appeared to delight in exposing, in all its unsavoriness, the nature of the "homo sensualis" and the less mentionable inclinations of the man-animal. They gloried in the beauties of the horrible and the pathetic, in death and in sin, and they talked with often incoherent sentimentality about the "noble bandit," the beauty of the Medusa, and the "fatal woman."[1] In a critical comment on these tendencies, Croce observes that the Romantics "lost sight of the true God" and subverted existing values where "lust and voluptuousness (were) put in place of ideals, (and) cruelty and horror (became) flavoured with sensual pleasure, a taste for incest, sadism, satanism and other amusements of that kind" (in Praz:xiii).

Further "proof" for the association of genius and madness was provided by the numerous instances of self-labeling, particularly common among the Romantic poets. These men of genius were among the first to suggest, in referring to themselves and other eminent individuals,

55

that the ancients were indeed correct in their assessment: the "demon of madness" was seen as more than just a stranger among their ranks. Schopenhauer could proclaim with confidence that "genius is nearer to madness than the average intelligence" (Sully, 1885:952), and find support for this pronouncement, not only among the ancients, but among such near contemporaries as Diderot (Sully, 1885:952), Lamartine (Radestock, 1884:1), Wieland (Radestock, 1884:1), Lenau (Radestock, 1884:54-55), Poe (Marks, 1926:22), and others. And while many of these modern "confessions" on the nature of genius were expressed in terms of the "inspired" madness of the ancients, the public, and particularly members of the medical professions, took the men of genius at their words—they clearly were not like ordinary men.

The issue of self-initiated labeling on the part of genius, and its relation to typing by others are the organizing concern of this chapter. While this examination is based not on the autobiographical accounts of the men of genius, but on the information provided by their labelers, the observations of the eminent individuals themselves were extensively quoted by these labelers and, therefore, constitute important data for this study. In the context of this discussion on self-labeling and its attendant effect on labeling by others, the positions of the two types of labelers, those who saw genius as madness and those who did not, will be examined to distinguish conditions for negative and positive typing.

The application of the term genius to "qualified" individuals during the eighteenth century marked the arrival of a new model for man. In antiquity, one had the sage, the poet, and the philosopher as the ideal; in the medieval period, there was the Christian saint; in the Renaissance, one finds the wit, the courtier, and the statesman. During the Enlightenment, it was the genius who was raised to an ideal of personality and, to a degree, retained this distinction throughout most of the nineteenth century. This development was to have serious implications for the social order and the existing system of stratification.

Generally deprived of wealth or a privileged class status, men of genius (or those who aspired to be such) tended to challenge the existing hierarchical order by substituting innate creative ability as a superior criterion for the evaluation of men. D'Alembert, an Enlightenment spokesman for the man of letters, recognized three factors separating men: birth, wealth, and intelligence—but only intelligence was deemed worthy of true esteem. Unlike the others, he argued, intelligence is a dependable national "resource," by its nature inexhaustible and incapable of being "taken" from its possessors (*Oeuvres Complètes De D'Alembert,* IV:354). Henri de Saint-Simon, writing a few years after the demise of the Ancien Régime, was less guarded in his vision of the future society—it was to be dominated by men of genius: the scientists, the artists, the men of ideas. In fact, he cautioned the power holders and the propertied classes not to impede the geniuses' quest for power, "great prestige," and money. Failure to comply with this warning, he feared, would lead to almost certain extinction of the members of the ruling elites. "To be convinced of the truth of what I have said," he argued, "you have only to reflect on the course of events in France since 1789" (1803:3). The final victory of the intellectual elite, according to Saint-Simon, is inevitable. Not only do these intellectuals march "beneath the banner of human progress" (1803:2) but, more importantly, they are skilled at mobilizing public opinion on their behalf. He counseled the established interests accordingly—the only prudent course is to "allow yourselves the merit of doing with a good grace what the scientists, artists and men of liberal ideas, allied with the have-nots, will sooner or later compel you to do" (1803:4).

The period of reaction to all "revolutionary" ideas initiated by Napoleon's defeat and the creation of the Quadruple Alliance meant, of course, that prospects to establish intelligence as a foremost legitimate criterion for the ranking of men had received a serious setback. The Metternich era refused to comply with the demands of this new, self-appointed intellectual aristocracy. Indeed, the events of the late eighteenth and early nineteenth centuries had made the position of this aspiring group rather precarious. The disappearance of the traditional "sponsor" class—the nobility and the aristocratized bourgeoisie—and the subsequent hazards of commercialization and the modern market place, left the status of the man of genius in question.[2] Generally impoverished and deprived of political power throughout most of the nineteenth century, the aspiring artist and man of ideas felt himself consumed by the anonymous masses.

The idea of madness remained as one existing alternative to define the man of genius as separate, unique, and divinely chosen. The aura of madness served the function of differentiating genius from the mean, the mediocre, or the bourgeois. "Many men of genius themselves prize madness and insanity as the highest distinction of the exceptional man" (1931:4), observed Kretschmer, for "the mentally normal man is, according to the conception itself, identical with the typical man, the average man, the philistine" (1931:6). This theme of the "blessed-ness" of madness is clearly reflected in Poe's "Eleanora":

> I am come of a race noted for vigor of fancy and ardor of passion. Men have called me mad; but the question is not yet settled, whether madness is or is not the loftiest intelligence; whether much that is glorious, whether all that is profound, does not spring from disease of thought. [in Marks:22]

Similarly, the poet Wieland spoke of the "amiable insanity of the Muses" (in W. Hirsch:71), and the clergyman Henry Ward Beecher commented on the desirability of at least some degree of madness (in Sanborn:188). Coleridge, in a defense of Swedenborg, proposed that, unlike ordinary madness, his was the madness of genius—"a madness, indeed, celestial, and glowing from a divine mind" (in Sanborn:154).

This emphasis on madness enabled gifted individuals and their ad-mirers to establish the men of genius as the modern heirs of the ancient Greek poets and seers. Like his predecessors, the man of genius could claim some of the powers and privileges granted the "fool," the "pos-sessed" prophet, or the mutilated priest. Recognized as the possessor of a "greater" truth, the "inspired" man of genius could counsel kings and "blaspheme" with impunity. However, it was not sufficient to claim that the mark of genius was a form of madness or demonic pos-session. As in classical times, the state of inspired mania was, in addi-tion, defined as an Olympian gift extended only to a special kind of being. The genius was like no other man: his uniqueness was founded not on quantitative, but qualitative differences; his ability to experience unusual states of mind responsible for profound creativity was rooted in his peculiar relation to the divine, and in a constitution that differed from that of ordinary men.

The conception of the divinely inspired sage and poet, encountered among the ancient Greeks and repopularized by the Romantics in reference to genius, conceives of the extraordinary man as an appointee of the supernatural entrusted with the furtherance of a divine plan. Diderot, commenting on a belief held by numerous men of genius, ob-served that "they themselves fancy that some god-like being rises up within them, seeks them out and uses them" (in Kretschmer, 1931:4). Similarly, observed Goethe, the work of a genius is "related to the daemonical, which does with him whatever it pleases, overwhelmingly, and to which he unconsciously surrenders, while believing he is acting on his own initiative" (in Tsanoff, 1949:2). Supportive of this view of genius was the Romantic belief that the work of God was left un- finished and in a perpetual state of unfolding, striving toward per- fection. It is in this sense that the man of genius was said to serve as an "Erlösungskraft" or force of redemption, as a "renovator" of the world, as one who "improves" upon the works of God. Commenting on the role of genius in furthering nature's "impulse towards perfection," Türck (1896:37) quoted approvingly from Schopenhauer:

> The actual objects are almost always very imperfect copies of the Ideas expressed in them; therefore the man of genius requires imagination in order to see things, not that which Nature has actually made, but which she endeavored to make, yet could not because of the conflict of her forms among themselves.

As the possessor of some essential "Urwahrheit" or primal truth, the man of genius, argued Türck, is impelled by his "inmost nature" to relentlessly "turn towards that which is divine and perfect. . . . Like the eagle soaring upwards to the sun, the man of genius strives to reach the light of knowledge, truth, life and perfection" (1896:197).

This essentially Romantic interpretation of genius as a product of supernatural causes was quite compatible with the idea that there is a distinction between the genius and the man of talent, a separation in- troduced during the mid-eighteenth century and continued into the current century.[3] Central to this distinction is the claim that genius is principally inborn or congenital, whereas talent is the consequence of learning and education. Unlike genius, which is inventive and newly creative, talent is defined as limited to imitation and the synthesis of existing knowledge. While genius is said to manifest itself spontaneously and with little effort, talent requires a high degree of labor and per- severance. A typical comparison between genius and talent is provided by Schwarz (1916):

> The achievements of the talented men are conscious, anticipated, slightly original, voluntary; the creations of the genius are semi- conscious, inspirational, spontaneous, highly original. [14]

> [Unlike talent] true genius . . . attains many-sided results in a comparatively short time, with comparatively little labor, with comparatively simple tools or apparatus, without premeditation, without perseverance conscious of its particular aim. [18]

The discrimination between genius and talent was intended, no doubt, to accentuate the extraordinary character of the former. Expanding the mystical and semireligious aura assigned by the Romantics, the man of genius became qualitatively set apart from the rest of mankind; he appeared to embrace the inexplicable.[4] Closely related to this image of the genius is the notion of divine inspiration or mania. The idea of "possession" served to embellish the magical quality assigned to genius and simultaneously heighten the distinctiveness of the exceptional man. Only the qualitatively distinct man of genius is capable of attaining the inspired madness of which the ancients had sung and, while in this state of excitation, only he is granted a glimpse of a greater truth. In short, the state of inspired madness is an integral part of a romantic and mystical conception of genius.

Almost inevitably, the question about the relation of divine madness to clinical insanity eventually arose. The men of genius, when they addressed this issue at all, did not, as a rule, express themselves definitively on this point. Like Lamartine, many argued that "genius carries in itself the principle of destruction, of death, of madness like a fruit carries a worm" (Sully, 1885:952). The frequently observed eccentricities of particularly the Romantics perpetuated beliefs like Pascal's that "the extreme mind is neighbor to extreme madness" (in Sully: 952). Similarly, the claim that the genius was like no ordinary man and produced his works in mysterious ways suggested to many, and particularly the medically trained professional, that genius was indeed akin to clinical insanity. The supposed spontaneity, involuntariness, and semiconsciousness of intellectual production—underscored in the very distinction between genius and talent, and testified to by men of genius[5] — supported the notion that profound intellectual creations are products of minds somehow unbalanced, even diseased. The man of talent, in comparison, with clearly inferior acumen, possessed a mind that appeared to function in normal and predictable ways. Unlike genius, which was said to differ qualitatively from talent or marked ability, the boundary between talent and mediocrity was one only of degree (see N. Hirsch, 1931:38). The man of talent was not an intellectual superman "in touch" with the cosmic and social milieu; he was an average man with superior ability—and he was sane. The man of genius, however, defined as qualitatively distinct and subject to the vagaries and capriciousness of divine possession, could only be seen with difficulty as totally normal, totally sane. As Armstrong-Jones observed (1914:

161) in a comparison of genius and talent, the former is less stable and seems disposed to a "want of equilibrium":

> Talent connotes the possession of special aptitudes for some purpose, and implies education. It is very much the result of memory and, as in Macaulay, it was the ready and responsive reaction to education and training. . . . Talent implies discrimination and a talented person is usually clever, and of good judgment; a genius is often erratic, unreliable, unstable, and irresponsible— George Morland, Robert Burns, Byron, Chatterton, Edgar Allen Poe are cases in point. Many of these and others of their kind betray a real want of equilibrium. They are dreamers and persons incapable of appreciating circumstances at their proper value and incapable of finding opportune adaptations.

A similar assessment is encountered in Kretschmer (1931:17), who regards the mystical or demonic component in genius as a primary source of pathology:

> To straightforward talent there must be added, to make genius, this 'daemon,' and it seems that the daemon, the inner voice, is founded in the psychopathic element. For the daemonical, which is the essence of genius, embraces the inexplicable, the spiritually creative and original and the whole gamut of strange passions and uncommon ideas.

The claim, then, that the genius serves as an agent for the supernatural, or acts on behalf of some greater cosmic vision, and the assertion that he differs in qualitative or generic terms from other humans, became two arguments supportive of the view that saw the man of genius as mentally unstable and diseased. And, indeed, those monographs in this study that adopt a pro-pathology judgment on genius are distinguished by the fact that, generally, one or both of these arguments are supported, or else tacitly accepted and left unchallenged. By comparison, in those assessments that project the view of the sane genius, the pronounced tendency is to challenge the view of the divine nature of genius and to argue that the genius differs from other persons only in the power of normal mental processes and the relatively perfection of normal human attributes. Constable (1905:105) captured what deserves to be called the "rational" view of genius when he wrote: "I deny the miraculous in genius; it is nothing more than a very exceptional deviation from the average." The disavowal of the magical and the qualitative difference defining genius is even encountered in six out of nine of those writings on genius that do not address the madness question.[6] Of those seven monographs that define genius as healthy and sane and were written between 1920 and 1950, for example, all challenge the romantic or mystical view of genius.[7] For the same time period, only two of the thirteen statements that judge genius as pathological are clearly characterized by a rational view of genius; the rest subscribe to the romantic interpretation.[8]

The rational view of genius, identified most closely with the anti-pathology position, is characterized by the absence of the traditional distinction between genius and talent. Assessing this distinction as imprecise and misleading, the term "genius" is either totally rejected (Hollingworth) or used interchangeably with talent (Oden, Terman, Ward), ability (Carroll, Cooley, Cox), intellect (Hock, 1949), intelligence (Carroll, Oden, Terman), and "the gifted" (Burks). More important than a mere change in terminology, however, is the emphasis on the idea that environmental factors are involved in the making of genius. While the role of "natural ability" or hereditary "potential" continues to be stressed in these writings, the recognition of the importance of social factors for mental development implies a challenge to the theory of the "born" genius.

The premise that individuals with a potential for extraordinary ability are quite common differed sharply from the prevailing romantic view on genius. To the objection that genius is encountered most infrequently in the population, and especially in the lower classes,[9] it was argued that unfavorable historical, social, and economic conditions have effectually contained the development of natural ability. Particularly the lower classes, argued Constable (1905:29), have had to suffer from the "swamping effect of poverty on achievement." Burst the environmental restraints upon ability, observed Ward (1906:237), and "the human mind will soar. The artificial classes of society possess no monopoly of the mental powers of man, and they seem to do so only because their economic, social, and educational environment enables them to rise into a freer intellectual atmosphere." Quoting from John M. Robertson, Ward concurred (1906:145): "We are driven back once more to the conclusion that potential genius is probably about as frequent in one class as in the other, and that it emerges in the ratio of its total opportunities." Because, in this view, geniuses are always those mentally endowed individuals granted the opportunity to develop their talents, the lessons for society are simple—to detect and promote the development of natural ability wherever it is encountered. As Harold Benjamin observes in the editor's introduction to Carroll's *Genius In The Making* (1940:xi), "To recognize outstanding ability and to develop it to its utmost is a chief task of this education. The present volume offers valuable aid to all parents and teachers who wish to perform this crucial task well."

Logically consistent with this rational view of genius is the accompanying demystification of the act of intellectual and artistic creation. Whereas in the romantic interpretation the creations of genius are said to proceed effortlessly and semiconsciously in a state of inspiration, the rational view stresses the normalcy and naturalness of the mental processes involved. Typical of this view is Dilthey's assertion (1886:28) that the great "Einbildungskraft" or power of imagination characteristic of genius is subject to the same mental and "psychological laws" encountered in normal men. Commenting critically on the supposed ease and suddenness of discovery in men of genius, Hock (1949) proposes an explanation that underscores the gradualness and deliberate nature of intellectual activity:

> Such uncontrollable tales as the one that the observation of a falling apple sufficed for Newton to find his famous law gravely distort the real state of affairs and are apt to support the erroneous belief that intuition originates all of a sudden. [31]

> In the crystallization of intuition the opportunity for repetition, for the thinking-out of a given subject plays a considerable part. [33]

> Every new repetition of a complicated situation finds the brain better prepared than on the previous occasion, thanks to preceding attempts at grasping the connections. An insignificant circumstance, left unobserved on the first occasion, or possibly not even present at that time, may then suffice to release intuition. [35]

The rational view on genius, then, rejects the sharp distinction between genius and talent and conceives of both as superior but, nevertheless, normal natural abilities that are subject, for their development, to favorable historical and social conditions. This interpretation of genius, while it had its early spokesmen in Helvetius and Condorcet, never enjoyed a majority consensus (see Ward, 1906:247-248). This appears somewhat surprising, especially with regard to the Enlightenment. It should be remembered that this period saw the rise of not only a democratic ideology, but the development of a theory of mind, identified with Locke and others, that stressed the extrinsic nature of all intelligence.[10] Accordingly, the mind of man was portrayed as a "tabula rasa" at birth with all existing intellectual differences in adult humans explained as the consequence of learning. It is interesting that, with the exception of Helvetius and Condorcet, the Enlightenment largely ignored the implications of "tabula rasa" for genius, while retaining the centrality of education for the making of talent and the intellectual growth of average men. No doubt, this seeming paradox must be seen as an attempt at raising the status of genius and providing a justification for granting special rights and privileges to the often precariously situated man of genius. Similarly, the sacred quality assigned to genius by the Romantics was designed to underscore the claims on behalf of genius as legitimate and deserving of special attention. But central to this mystical view on genius, a view derived from antiquity, were such classical notions as the "demon," divine possession, and the melancholic temperament—all potentially suggestive of a precarious state of mind. And far from trying to clear himself of any association with clinical madness, the man of genius testified, not infrequently, to the marginality of his mental health. Commenting on the delicate constitution of especially the poetic genius, Eckermann described the views of Goethe: "The extraordinary performed by such people [the geniuses] . . . necessitates a particularly delicate organization in order to be capable of the rarer perceptions and be susceptible to the voice of heaven"[11] (in Möbius, I, 1909:159). Particularly hazardous to the mental health of genius, observed Goethe, is the tendency of genius to stand in frequent opposition to the existing order. Given the delicateness of his constitution, the price exacted for this opposition is the frequent deterioration in his mental and physical condition (in Möbius, I, 1909:159-160).[12]

It seems clear that the association of genius with madness, an association that has held the rank of scientific fact during the nineteenth and much of the twentieth century, is, in no small measure, the result of pronouncements made in support of this association by numerous men of genius. And even though many of these pronouncements were made in more general than specific terms and were in reference to divine mania, these proved difficult to ignore, especially in view of the near absence of statements to the contrary. As has been argued in this chapter, the genius tended to promote a romantic interpretation of the great man that contained the idea of madness or divine possession as an integral part. Faced with a generally pronounced self-indictment by the men of genius, it appeared not unreasonable to openly associate genius with a form of clinical pathology. It is interesting to observe that in nearly all monographs in this study that defined genius as pathological, the pronouncements of distinguished men are extensively cited and constitute a central part of the pro-madness argument.[13] Typical of this tendency is Sully, who provided the following evaluation (1885: 952):

> Against the compact consensus of opinion on the one side we have only a rare protest like that of Charles Lamb on behalf of the radical sanity of genius. Such a mass of opinion cannot lightly be dismissed as valueless. It is impossible to set down utterances of men like Diderot or Goethe to the envy of mediocrity. Nor can we readily suppose that so many penetrating intellects have been misled by a passion for startling paradox. We are to remember, moreover, that this is not a view of the great man "ab extra," like that of the vulgar already referred to; it is the opinion of members of the distinguished fraternity themselves who are able to observe and study genius from the inside.

What was commonly known in the second half of the nineteenth century and, therefore, did not need mentioning was the observation that Charles Lamb, the sole voice cited in defense of the sanity of genius, had himself been institutionalized in an asylum. Most were familiar with Carlyle's charge of Lamb's "diluted insanity" (in Sanborn, 1886:114). The dearth of testimonials on behalf of sanity proved a serious disadvantage to those who challenged the view of the mad genius. The acknowledgment of this fact, while perhaps dictated by scholarly ethics, could do little to strengthen one's argument, as evidenced by Stevenson's unintended paradox (1887:670): "Charles Lamb, himself at times oppressed with mental gloom, stands almost alone in defense of 'the sanity of true genius.' With this view [Lamb's] I am in accord.

The association of genius and madness was, by this time, firmly established in the minds of many. Even the "victims," the men of genius themselves, provided few effective counter-arguments. Indeed, they often lent support and credence to the charge.

NOTES

1. For an excellent exposition of these tendencies see Mario Praz, *The Romantic Agony*, 1951.

2. For a discussion of the plight of the French man of letters during the nineteenth century, see Céasar Graña's *Bohemian Versus Bourgeois*, 1964.

3. This distinction, while introduced by Condillac and others in the mid-seventeen hundreds, was sharpened into a strong antithesis during the Romantic's "Storm and Stress" period (see Wittkower, 1973: 305).

4. William James reflects this point of view when he commented on the origin of genius: "The causes of the production of great men lie in a sphere wholly inaccessible to the social philosopher. He must simply accept geniuses as data, just as Darwin accepts his spontaneous variations" (in Royse, 1891:20).

5. The issue of spontaneity and compulsiveness in genius will be examined in future pages.

6. See Cahan (1911), Constable (1905), Cooley (1897), Jsenburg (1936), Ward (1906), and Zilsel (1918, 1926).

7. See Burks (1930), Carroll (1940), Cox (1926), Hock (1920, 1949), Hollingworth (1926), Oden (1947), and Terman (1925).

8. It is interesting to observe that the two "dissenters" in this group to subscribe to a rational view of genius are Lange-Eichbaum (1927, 1930) and Jaspers (1926), both identified earlier as forerunners of the labeling perspective.

9. The issue that genius is encountered most frequently in the privileged classes was initiated by Galton's formulation of the hereditary nature of genius in 1869 (see Galton, 1962).

10. For John Locke's famous attack on "innate ideas" see his *An Essay Concerning Human Understanding,* a book that became, according to Carl L. Becker, the "psychological gospel of the eighteenth century" (C. Becker, 1969:64).

11. Translated by this author.

12. This view of Goethe's is consistent with the Romantic idea of "Weltschmerz," a term used to convey the mood of sentimental sadness and mental depression to which the genius, far more than ordinary men, was believed susceptible. Defined as the possessor of some greater truth, the genius was seen as driven to this mood of depression by comparing the actual state of the world with that of his ideal vision (see Hagen, 1877:659-660).

The mental state beyond this melancholic depression was total insanity, a condition believed to bring relief from the agonies of "Weltschmerz." Note Byron's wish for deliverance: "I have also wished for insanity—for anything to quell memory, the never-dying worm that feeds on my heart" (in Sanborn, 1886: 126).

13. In the antimadness assessments, the self-definitions by geniuses as mad are generally ignored or else discarded as having been made with the aims of rhetorical beauty rather than scientific truth.

The Fear of Madness

A Consequence of the Romantics' Redefinition of Genius

Like death and suffering, the topic of madness proved an irresistable source of fascination for the genius, and especially the Romantic poets and artists. Not only did it provide, in the observation of Shelley, an "admirable dramatic and poetical" subject for literature (in Sanborn: 134), but, quite importantly, this preoccupation testified to something else—a sense of foreboding nourished by the suspicion that the nature of true genius indeed contained the ingredients for total madness. This fear of becoming clinically ill is captured by Byron. While often appearing to revel in a professed madness, he, nevertheless, spoke with considerable apprehension about his future: "I picture myself slowly expiring on a bed of torture, or terminating my days like Swift—a grinning idiot" (in Sanborn:126).

It has been argued in the previous chapter that the self-labeling of the genius was motivated by considerations that were self-serving in nature. This generalization must now be qualified. While the idea of "mania" was part of a romantic interpretation of the great man and, therefore, the notions of "Weltschmerz" and divine inspiration affirmed one's membership in the "touchy" tribe of genius, there was a lingering suspicion that the sufferings of full-scale insanity were inevitable. The admission of madness and the expressed fear of going mad was more than the willful projection of an ideal image; it was rooted in a system of premises and a sense of logic to which the man of genius unwittingly contributed.

Prior to the eighteenth century, the period when the term "genius" acquired its modern meaning, it was commonly accepted that the human imagination, or fancy, constitutes a capricious and dangerous element in the lives of men. Recognized as the fountainhead of original creativity, it was simultaneously admired and feared. Pascal, writing towards the middle of the seventeenth century, reflects this ambivalence clearly:

> Imagination—It is this dominant part in man, this mistress of error and falsity, and more often trickster than not. . . . But being most often false, it gives no mark of its quality, marking the true and the false with the same nature.[1] [*Pensées et Opuscules,* 1968:362-363]

To benefit from imagination and yet contain its great potential for disaster and evil meant, as Pascal cautioned those who were the "wisest of men," that one had to consciously "resist" its intoxicating powers with all one's strength.[2] It is not surprising, therefore, that during the 1700s, when the genius became recognized as a model of a superior man, the nature of genius was defined in a way that virtually precluded victimization by his own fancy. In the typical Enlightenment explication of genius—e.g., Gerard, Duff, and others (see Fabian, 1966:IX-XLVII)—the imagination was seen as contrained by a number of "powers" or faculties" recognized as particularly developed in the great man. Indispensable to the harmonious interplay of mental powers was the faculty of judgment, or reason, which in conjunction with memory, taste, sense, sensibility, and the like averted not only "caprice" and "extravagance," but, as Gerard observed (1974:73-74), made "madness and frenzy" a near impossibility for genius.

The Romantics, seeming to disregard the warnings of their predecessors, supplanted the Enlightenment conception of the creative man with one that granted the imagination a clear predominance over judgment.[3] Like the Schlegels, Lessing, and others (see Nordau, 1900:73; also Cahan, 1911:32-38), Schiller proposed that a consciously applied faculty of reason, far from being beneficial, would serve to impede the aesthetic imagination and forestall the most profound creations:

> It is not well in works of creation that reason should too closely challenge the ideas that come thronging to the doors. Taken by itself, an idea may be highly unsuitable, even venturesome, and yet in conjunction with others, themselves equally absurd alone,

it may furnish a suitable link in the chain of thought. Reason can not see this. . . . In a creative brain reason has withdrawn her watch at the doors, and ideas crowd in pell-mell. [in W. Hirsch: 31]

To suspend the "laws of rationally thinking reason," which was a Romantic dictum particularly aimed at the artistic and poetic genius, meant, as the Schlegels observed, to be transported "into the lovely vagaries of fancy and the primitive chaos of human nature" (in Nordau: 73). That the reference to the "primitive chaos of human nature" was meant to encompass a variety of states of mind, including, importantly, the possibility of madness, can safely be assumed. Coleridge, another Romantic, commented specifically on the dire consequences of a suspended judgment:

The reason may resist for a long time . . . but too often, at length, it yields for a moment, and the man is mad forever. . . . I think it was Bishop Butler who said that he was all his life struggling against the devilish suggestions on his senses, which would have maddened him if he had relaxed the stern wakefulness of his reason for a single moment. [in Sanborn: 139]

While it is true that the Romantics had helped to promote a mystical view of genius, one that contained the concept of divine mania, it nevertheless would be wrong to assume that the attack on reason had been designed chiefly to link genius with "mania." More importantly, the criticism of judgment and, to a lesser degree, sense, taste, and memory—the "rational" counterweights to imagination—served as a proclamation of independence from the traditional constraints and the authority of the academies; it was seen as the primary means for the attainment of originality, particularly with reference to literature and the arts.[4] The dominant Enlightenment view of the genius as an educated individual whose abundant imagination was properly tempered by good taste, training in the classics, and an appreciation for the masters, proved unacceptable to the Romantic spirit. The objective of expressing the original—which was, after all, by definition the mark of the true genius—could be best maximized by near or total disregard for the authorities and the traditional forms. In the absence of such freedom, the exceptional man would be reduced to imitation and a synthesis of existing knowledge, a characteristic that defined not the genius but the mere man of talent.[5] Hence, the proposed argument that genius is characterized as the imagination working alone and unfettered, rather than as a synthesizing of mental agents, deserves to be seen as an attempt by the Romantics to provide a new explanation, or model, aimed at understanding the "true" nature of the creative man.

Given the commonality of the belief concerning the relation of sanity and the synthesis of mental faculties, the Romantic reformulation established a logical foundation for the association of genius with madness. Indeed, the Romantics, trapped by their premises and system of logic, began to suspect the inevitable. The expressed fear of going mad and the frequency of self-labeling (usually in a general reference to genius) suggest that the genius fell victim to his own sense of logic—one that appeared to dictate that sooner or later he would succumb to the "demon of madness." However, not all creative individuals would need to fear equally for their sanity. The Romantic redefinition of genius was directed primarily at poets and artists; they, more than others, were seen as dependent on a bountiful imagination and, as such, were most susceptible to madness. Clemens Brentano, an intimate of Goethe commented on the dangers of poetry: "It is really a suspicious thing to be a poet by profession; one who lives from poetry has lost his balance; an oversized goose liver, regardless how tasty, presupposes always a diseased goose" (in Noack:249).[6] Similarly, Poe recognized the link between insanity and the unbridled imagination of the poet when one of his characters acknowledged that, "I am come of a race noted for vigor of fancy and ardor of passion. Men have called me mad" (in Marks:22).

The argument that sanity presupposes the harmonious interplay of mental powers, far from losing its appeal throughout the nineteenth century, served to support the "scientific" claims of the madness-genius association.[7] Those who endorsed this argument typically and predictably stressed the greater susceptibility of the aesthetic genius.[8] But while the poet, the artist, and the composer proved most vulnerable to the charge of madness, a slim prospect for sanity was generally held out for them. Mental health could be exacted at a price—a high one for artists—the containment of imagination. This placed the aesthetic individual in a serious dilemma, for, as Sanborn observed (1886:147), "The same faculty leads us to glory or throws us into a cell of a lunatic asylum. It is visionary imagination which forges the phantoms of the madman and creates the personages of an artist." Hence, the deliberate imposition of limits on one's imagination, while it served to promote sanity, meant the likely obstruction of creative energies. Only the strongest and most determined could fare well in the battle for sanity and genuine artistic expression. The wild rovings of the poet's and artist's fancy were not easily subdued and necessitated, as Coleridge had cautioned, the stern and unrelenting "wakefulness" over the imagination.

In view of these professed difficulties, it is not surprising that those who stressed the pathological nature of the great man only recognized the existence of a handful of totally sane geniuses and, even less frequently, sane aesthetic geniuses. The number of the great aesthetics was typically confined to men such as Shakespeare, Goethe, Leonardo da Vinci, Michelangelo, and occasionally others who were assessed to be of similar stature.[9] Quite commonly, what was seen as the key to their sanity was recognized as a state of balance, or the harmonious functioning of mental powers. W. Hirsch (1897:58), for example, in reference to Goethe and Mozart, observed that their fancy was "directed by a high intellectual faculty which checked its boiling over, held the ideas to an ordered sequence, and eliminated disturbing elements." To Noack (1859:249), similarly, the mental health of Goethe, Shakespeare, and Schiller was seen as founded on their ability to dilute dangers of a poetic existence through their involvement in other, more rational enterprises: the study of history, languages, and the natural sciences.

The appeal of the argument that the totally sane genius is one who derives benefits from not one, but various key faculties, meant that many of those who challenged the pathology position on genius felt compelled, nevertheless, to accept the definition of sanity.[10] Health and sanity, they confirmed, is not found in the disproportionate exercise of a single faculty, but necessitates balance and equilibrium. But, unlike the more typical pathology argument of the great man—which embraced the Romantics' redefinition of genius and, from it, derived the logical conclusion—these pro-sanity statements flatly reject the Romantic formulation. The true nature of genius, it was argued, is not sustained by an overpowering imagination; more correctly, it is defined by the fortunate arrangement of various intellectual agents. Reminiscent of Gerard and the Enlightenment, for example, is Stevenson's attempt (1887) to once again confer reason as a natural attribute of genius:

Imagination, however bold may be its flight, is, nevertheless, under the restraining influence of reason, and performs its wondrous work along true parallels of thought. [664]

That genius "has its roots in a nervous organization of exceptional delicacy," is undoubtedly true, but it does not necessarily follow that the liability to mental discord and confusion is thereby increased, because this delicacy of brain-structure and its function are admirably adjusted, and the very perfection of the mechanism enables it to work with least possible friction or injury. [672]

It was not sufficient, however, merely to reject as a falsity the Romantics' premise regarding the nature of the great man. Too numerous were the testimonies of persons judged to be geniuses, who endorsed the primacy of imagination and commented on the precariousness of their own state of health. In the absence of an equally impressive list of supporting testimonies, a viable defense for the sanity of genius required more than mere denial or a modification in logic—it needed more "reliable" empirical data that could withstand scientific scrutiny.

A solution, adopted in eight of fifteen pro-sanity statements in this study, was to dismiss the genius as an authority on his own condition—the utterances of eminent men on the nature of genius were judged unreliable. The next step was to submit geniuses directly to medical and psychological testing.[11] However, while Zola consented, in the interest of science, to an examination by fifteen psychiatrists, it does not appear that many others were willing to do so. An alternative was to confine these clinical tests to "gifted children," defined by their examiners as young geniuses based on performances on intelligence tests. While this approach was open to the charge that it did not study the genius proper, these young "geniuses" were relatively willing subjects and could be studied in sufficient numbers to meet statistical requirements.[12]

A primary aim of these clinical studies was to discredit the testimonies of genius and, specifically, to disprove the claim that a genius was a "victim" of his imagination. Hoesch-Ernst, for example, in his discussion of a child prodigy of music, stressed the conclusion that the child appeared inherently drawn to the "logical" and "proportional;" in music, he displayed a preference for the "classical" and shunned all "emotionalism" and "sentimentality." It was suggested that all preferences for "dark feelings" and sentimentality on the part of genius are the consequence of educational practices (1909:678-679). Similarly,

Toulouse, one of the fifteen examiners of Zola, rejects the Romantic interpretation of genius. He observed (1896:281), "What seems to me to be the most immediate cause of intellectual superiority is the fortunate arrangement of all the faculties which permits their best utilization." Confirming the mental health of Zola, he recognized this health to reside in his "superior forms of intelligence which constitute judgment, imagination and will" (1896:279-280).

Toulouse, however, represented a minority viewpoint. Of the fifteen psychiatrists who examined Zola, the majority concluded "that his genius had its source in the the neurotic elements of his temperament" (Trilling:163). This view, perhaps, falls short of seeing the subject as totally mad, but the idea of seeing genius springing from "neurotic elements" definitely implies that the root of genius is imbedded in the irrational faculties. The "scientific" conclusion of the majority did not, as some had hoped, go far toward discrediting the self-indicting statements of the men of genius. And Zola, as a man of genius, did little to discredit their findings—as a matter of fact, he concurred with them completely.

In retrospect, however, this could not be unexpected. It has been seen that self-labeling by the men of genius served to provide recognition of special status and the freedom from conventional restraints that attended it. It has also been seen that the association of madness and genius grew out of the changed definition of genius in the Romantic period, which inevitably became applied to unchanged ideas about the nature of sanity. Finally, the men of genius, themselves partially responsible for their own characterization, could do little else but admit the obvious—clinical madness was a likely, if not inevitable, end of their condition.

NOTES

1. Translated by Anne McGovern.

2. "Imagination has great influence," observed Pascal. "How will we profit from that? By following this influence . . . ? No. But by resisting it" (*Pensées*: 370).

3. Of particular interest is Kant, who, in an early explication of his genius concept, clearly cautioned his contemporaries against the danger of unbridled imagination. He observed: "To free imagination from this constraint and to allow one's peculiar talent to rove about in wild disorder, contrary to the laws of Nature, might betoken, perhaps, a great original madness" (in W. Hirsch:40). Yet.

some twenty years later, in a restatement of his earlier position, he stressed the supremacy of fancy and applied the term genius to only those greats with an aesthetic orientation (see Hagen: 652).

4. As Wittkower observed (1973: 298), the Romantics' fight for liberation from the collective discipline of the academies indeed "fostered a great richness and variety of personal styles and enhanced the potentiality of unpredictable and sudden changes."

5. This fervent advocacy of originality and the inviolability of the individual was rooted in the Romantic's conviction that genuine creativity, especially in art, is not teachable (see Wittkower, 1973: 298).

6. Translated by the author.

This does not mean that Brentano regarded Goethe as mad, for, unlike some others, he did not "live from poetry" alone, but engaged in a variety of enterprises.

And as Merk, another intimate of Goethe, had observed, what made Goethe different from most other poets was his deliberate struggle not to succumb to a "one-sided, subjective phantasy life," but to be in compliance with the "real world" (in Noack: 249-250).

7. It is not suggested that this constitutes the only, or even the dominant view of mental health throughout the nineteenth and twentieth centuries. It is merely one explanation that, particularly in the former century, retained its popularity with regard to the man of genius. The charge of a faulty or overactive imagination constitutes a central argument in the writings of Lélut (1836, 1846), Moreau (1859), Noack (1859), Radestock (1884), and W. Hirsch (1897). In many others this theme constitutes a supportive or secondary argument. Lombroso, for instance, a chief exponent of the degeneracy statement, expands the consequences of an unstable equilibrium to include a criminal disposition for especially the nonscientific genius:

> Among poets and artists criminality is, unfortunately well marked. Many among them are dominated by passion which becomes the most powerful spur of their activity; they are not protected by the logical criticism and judgment with which men of science are armed. [1891:59]

8. Moreau is somewhat unusual in his insistence that genius always functions in the absence of reason and believes "totally what imagination suggests to it" (Moreau, 1859:497). Generally, one distinguished between aesthetic and other geniuses in their degree of "victimization" by their fancy.

9. It should not be assumed, however, that there was total consensus with regard to even these few individuals.

10. This tendency is especially pronounced in an anonymous statement (1861), Dilthey (1886), Stevenson (1887), Toulouse (1896), Hoesch-Ernst (1909) and Hock (1949).

11. Specifically, see Toulouse (1896), Hoesch-Ernst (1909), Terman (1925), Hollingworth (1926), Cox (1926), Burks (1930), Carroll (1940), and Oden and Terman (1947).

12. When, as in the case of Hollingworth, the term genius is rejected, it is done not to underscore differences between these young subjects and "true" adult geniuses, but to suggest that the term itself is misleading and has lost its scientific precision. This position served, not incidentally, to somewhat discredit the charge that "true" geniuses were not being studied.

Changing Conceptions of Man

The Man of Genius as a Victim of Biological Necessity

Talent is that which is in a man's power; Genius is that in whose power a man is.

[J. R. Lowell (in Moorman, 1940:IX)]

In the pre-Romantic conception of genius, the process of invention was typically attributed to the intimate relation of at least two dominant powers or agents—imagination and judgment. While the genius derived his vitality and originality from the partially subconscious and irrational workings of his imagination, he relied on a "sound and piercing judgment" to contain the ill-effects of this potentially hazardous power (Gerard: 71). Unlike the imagination, which was activated spontaneously and impulsively,[1] the exercise of judgment required conscious application; it was determination or will that helped to activate one's judgment and served to maximize its benefits. Therefore, while both imagination and judgment were seen as natural attributes of man, and believed particularly developed in the genius, the former was seen as spontaneous, while the sufficient utilization of the latter remained under the individual's control, and, hence, was problematic.[2] Expectedly, in recognition of the dangers of an untended imagination, the pre-Romantic examinations of genius were prone to urge, or even prescribe, the firm exercise of judgment. Gerard, Duff, Voltaire, and others argued, accordingly, that a fertile imagination "should" or "must" be attended by an active judgment (see Tonelli:294-296).[3] And if the genius did not adequately exercise his power of reason, his failure to do so, as one who is the "wisest" among men, was held to be particularly blameworthy. To allow one's imagination free rein and, in this way, become subject to a variety of dangers, including madness, testified not to an inherent weakness in one's genius, but to a lack of normal prudence and foresight. As George Rosen observes (1969:165) in his discussion of the prevailing view of insanity in seventeenth and eighteenth century Europe,

> Unreason, and with it insanity, were related primarily to the quality of volition and not to the integrity of the rational mind. Endowed with reason, man was expected to behave rationally, that is, according to accepted social standards. Rational choice was his to make by virtue of his nature. Eccentric or irrational behaviour, actions which diverged from accepted norms, were considered as rooted in error or as derangements of the will and therefore subject to correction.

The Romantics' departure from the rationalist tradition in the explanation of genius was to lead to a more deterministic conception of the great man. By proposing that the imagination was superior to and, even, incompatible with judgment and, therefore, should be allowed to produce free from all "artificial" constraints, the image of the creative process was to acquire a decidely compulsive and irrational characteristic. Dissuaded from exercising his judgment, taste, or memory, the genius would now be seen as submitting to the whims of his imagination; and, no longer a "master" over his imagination, he was now to become its "victim."

This view of the genius as dependent on an impulsive and dominant imagination, a view supported by the acceptance of the classical notion of demonic possession, suggested to the Romantics that the great man was, in fact, not subject to "normal" or "natural" mental processes; he produced semiconsciously in a state of inspiration—even against his will. The works of genius, proclaimed Schopenhauer, are the consequence of an inner or "instinctive necessity" and never the products of intention or choice (in N. Hirsch:291-292). And Goethe, in reference to his poetry, maintained that his most accomplished works were the result of "Zwangsdichten," an instinctive and invincible impulse to

express his ideas and feelings in poetic form (in Möbius, 1909:187-188).
In his *Tasso,* Goethe sketched a portrait of this creative impulse:

Alphonso: I beg of thee to break this hapit up!
            The poet's loss will be the man's success.

Tasso: I've struggled day and night against this need;
            I'm worn out trying to shut up my breast.
            'Tis useless! Sing I must; else life's not life.
            Prohibit the poor silkworm's industry
            On pain of death, yet still he'll keep right on
            Drawing the costly web from his entrails,
            Nor cease until his golden cerecloth's wove.

                              [Act V, scene 2
                              in W. Hirsch:43]

This essentially Romantic image of the extraordinary man as one
who creates his works from instinctive necessity was to become, quite
ironically, a primary basis for the "scientific" or "clinical" claims on
behalf of the genius-madness association. The willing acceptance of
this view of the great man, surprising at first, is best explained when
seen as rooted in a major shift in the conception of man. The neoclassical acceptance of the doctrine of free will, rejected by many
throughout the nineteenth and twentieth centuries as illusory, was
gradually replaced by the view that conceived of man as fundamentally
controlled—the true condition of man existed not in the exercise of
reason, freedom, and choice, but remained subject primarily to factors
beyond his control. What distinguished the genius, in this deterministic
conception of man, was that he, more than most others, was a victim
of necessity—a necessity dictated by his own particular constitution.

While it is not within the scope of this examination to explore the
various factors responsible for this shift in the general view of man,
one contributing development is relevant to this study. The quest for
legitimacy and respectability by leaders of the newly founded social
and psychological sciences, especially throughout the nineteenth century, proceeded from the assumption that these disciplines, comparable
to the natural sciences, were grounded in concrete and "scientific"
constraints or determinants (see Matza, 1964:Ch.I). All notions of
human freedom and reason were seen as essentially prescientific in
orientation and incompatible with the vigorous dictates of scientific
inquiry. If man possesses freedom and choice, observed Enrico Ferri,

a founder of the positivist school of criminology, social and psychological behavior cannot become a subject for scientific study:

> This moral liberty, if once admitted, would make all psychological and social science impossible and absurd in exactly the same way that the supposition of free choice in the atoms of matter would destroy all physical and chemical science. . . . Negation of free will is the necessary condition of all sociological theory and practice. [in Matza: 6-7] [4]

The developing behavioral sciences, therefore, were receptive to and helped foster a new image of man, one that was based on the negation of choice.[5] And, as Matza observes with regard to the deterministic tendencies in the social sciences during the nineteenth century:

> What better group to start with than criminals? Surely they did not possess reason. And to deny them freedom was not without its compensations. Indeed, the needs of the new scientific disciplines coincided with the preachings of compassionate humanitarianism. The negation of freedom not only suited the pretentions and ambitious of social science; it also was a fundamental requirement of a view that commanded the treatment of criminals. Persons without choice are not responsible for their actions. Instead of punishment, they require treatment or other forms of correction. [Matza: 7]

The criminal, however, was not alone in being defined as devoid of freedom and reason; the absence of self-determinism was seen as a condition that described the lunatic and man of genius as well. And while the madman's "unreason" seemed apparent from mere observation, the genius, like Lamartine, frequently testified to his own condition. "It is not I who thinks," proclaimed Lamartine, "my ideas think for me" (in Lombroso: 20). This self-view of the genius as a "victim" of his condition was most generally accepted throughout the course of the nineteenth century and the first half of the twentieth, particularly by those who were accustomed to dealing with man as a biologically constrained being—those trained in the medical sciences. The members of the medical professions—who, as we have seen, were those most likely to define genius as pathological—commonly accepted the Romantics' conception of the "natural" genius, but, unlike the Romantics, interpreted it in the context of the assumptions of biological constraint and causality.

Thus, it is the view of the genius as a victim of "instinctive necessity" that helped foster the claim, as expressed in the degeneracy argument, that the great man's "powerlessness to will" constitutes a pathological condition that is rooted in a biologically regressive organism (Nordau: 20). This "organic weakness of will" recognized in the genius, the lunatic, and the criminal alike, led to the assertion that all three are members of the same "anthropological family" in possession of nearly identical mental and somatic "stigmata" (Nordau: 22). Importantly, one of the chief nonphysical "brand-marks" shared by the "higher" and "lower" degenerates was the condition of emotional instability and the possibility of full-scale madness. The charge that all degenerates are subject to the condition of "moral insanity" rested on the assertion that the degenerate, due to some constitutional deficiency, lacks the necessary moral ingredient to impose limits on his thoughts and actions.[6]

Clearly, not all of those who endorsed the pathology position on genius did so from the perspective of the degeneracy argument. In these others, however, the "impulse" to produce is generally interpreted, similarly to the degeneracy argument, as a precariously unstable condition of mind that somehow has its origin in a uniquely constituted physico-neurological organism.[7] Typical of the proponents of this type of explanation is the physician-psychiatrist Jacques-Joseph Moreau, one of the first to base the genius-madness association on a review of the clinical histories of men of genius. Based on his examination, Moreau concurred with the Romantic view that the genius differs from most other men in the degree of involuntariness that characterizes his intellectual processes. "Contrary to what is observed in men of average intelligence," Moreau noted (1859:499) "the work of superior men is totally spontaneous and somehow as involuntary as possible."[8] Unlike the Romantic interpretation of the involuntary activity of mind, seen typically in terms of divine possession and conceived as evidence of the genius' mystical and divine origin, Moreau's "scientific" explanation stresses the physiological basis for this condition. The compulsiveness of genius, in Moreau's interpretation, is the result of a dangerous "mental erethism," a "morbid" nervous affliction akin to idiocy with clearly biological sources (Moreau: 465); the genius must follow the impulsive "bursts" of his imagination, since his "morbid" physiology prevents the exercise of will and reason (Moreau: 388-389)—"matter having conquered the mind, the individual from then on acts only by a kind of automation, without liberty, without conscience" (Moreau:401).[9] He quotes approvingly from R. Parise:

> There is something in the nerves, in the veins, in the blood, in the fibers of a man of genius, whoever he may be, scientist, artist, poet or mathematician, which pushes him to the exaggeration either of feeling, of ideas or of action. [Moreau:495-496][10]

In Moreau, then, an unbridled imagination continues to be treated— comparable to the seventeenth and eighteenth centuries—as the primary agent for the genius' undoing. What distinguishes his from the former discussions on genius is the markedly larger element of compulsiveness that is seen as dictated by a "morbid" physiology. In subsequent examinations, while the concept of a dominant imagination retained much of its popularity, it occasionally gave way to a new agent of coercion—a specifically identified power of instinct. This constitutes a variation on those explications where reference to "instinct" is made in a general way, designed to underscore the "inflamed" and spontaneous tendency of a prevailing imagination. In those instances where the term "instinct" is applied in reference to a concrete entity, such as in Stekel (1909, 1917), Freud (1957, 1958), and Hinkle (1923), the creative individual is seen as subject to a "surplus" libido, defined primarily as an overly active sexual impulse. Because the degree of libidinal vigor, in this view, remains essentially constant and commands satisfaction, the genius' options are few. He either succumbs to fixated infantile desires and, in this way, joins the ranks of criminals and perverts, or else he sublimates or rechannels his libidinal energies in pursuit of higher intellectual and aesthetic concerns. Therefore, while the genius, unlike Moreau's interpretation, appears to be less constrained by virtue of the option of substitute gratification, the sexual libido, nevertheless, is defined as strenuously resisting adaptation to societal demands. And indeed, to Stekel, the struggle inherent in the sublimation of libidinal impulses results inevitably in a disposition to neurosis.[11]

As has been seen, the spokesmen for the association of genius and madness endorsed, or at least tacitly accepted, the Romantics' belief in the genius' uncontrollable "state of inspiration." They differ from the Romantics by defining this state, unequivocally, as a clinically determinable aberration of the mind.[12] The substitution of "tangible" biological forces for the earlier "demons" and a generally mystical explanation was made possible, it is being argued, by the developing behavioral sciences that subscribed to a highly deterministic conception of man. And what distinguished the genius, in this view, was the "clinical" assessment that he, more than the average man, was subject to factors beyond his control.

In comparison, those who stressed the sanity of genius abstained from, or actively opposed, the assumption that the genius produces compulsively in a semiconscious state of inspiration.[13] They either stressed the essential "normalcy" of the mental processes involved, or else took such for granted. Accordingly, the genius is believed to be no more constrained than other men and, in this sense, is regarded as "master" over his condition. Hock (1949), for instance, addressing the issue of compulsiveness in genius, believed such to be the expression, not of an absence of will, but of precisely the opposite—an extraordinarily high degree of will power:

> [The genius] appears weak of will only whenever he does not choose to "will." In all acts pointed toward the goal of his "willing" he exerts the strength of an athlete, he manifests a willpower that does not tolerate any diversion. The most intense concentration is an indispensable prerequisite for the accomplishment of extraordinary achievement. [Hock, 1949:45-46]

By granting the genius a greater degree of freedom and choice, defined in the majority of pro-sanity statements as at least equal to that of other men, it became more difficult to regard the great man as a creature enslaved by heredity and destined for mental illness. In this, a more rationalistic interpretation of genius, far greater emphasis is assigned to the elements of learning and other particulars of the sociocultural environment. And while this shift in emphasis makes it possible, of course, to define the genius as a nearly total "victim" of his social environment, the ingredient of volition virtually precludes an equally one-sided sociological-determinist conception of the great man. The element of choice, in conjunction with a superior intellect, suggests a view of the genius as one who not only is able to adjust to the inadvertencies of his personal environment, but, indeed, is capable of the manipulation of that environment.

The view of the sane genius, which remained always a minority judgment throughout the period of the genius-madness controversy, gradually rose, as we have seen, to its greatest popularity during the 1920 to 1950 time span.[14] This development was contemporary with, and appears clearly related to, a general decline in the strict biological-determinist explanations of human behavior. As Matza (1964:7) has noted, what distinguishes the twentieth from the nineteenth century has been a gradual shift in the conception of man away from a "hard" determinism to a more "balanced" view that vacillates between the extreme alternatives of choice and constraint.

NOTES

1. To Voltaire, for example, the imagination functioned totally without "assistance from volition" (1901:159, 162). Gerard observed similarly that the "activity of fancy is like an internal stimulus, which will not allow genius to lie idle or dormant, but makes it operate spontaneously and with constancy" (Gerard:59).

2. Gerard, for example, while proclaiming that "the most luxuriant fancy stands most in need of being checked by judgment" (Gerard:75), acknowledged the possibility in genius of an imagination left unattended: "Judgment is of so great importance, that, though we must often acknowledge genius in works in which judgment has not been scrupulously exercised, yet, this circumstance never fails to render them far less valuable than they would have been, if they had been finished with correctness" (Gerard:74-75)

3. Note Voltaire's urging to exercise judgment (1901:166-167): "When imagination is remarkably stirring and ardent, it may easily degenerate into madness . . . (hence) this active imagination always requires the association of judgment." Gerard, similarly, argued that "so when it (imagination) exerts itself in the way of genius, it has an immediate connexion with judgment; which must constantly attend it, and correct and regulate its suggestions" (Gerard:37).

4. As Nisbet observed (1912:26) in his examination of genius and madness: "In the modern theory of brain-function . . . there is no place for that bugbear of the older metaphysicians, the will."

5. Spencerian sociology, Lombrosoian criminology, Watsonian behaviorism, and Pavlovian conditioning were all suggestive of determinism.

6. As Nisbet observed (1912:27): "It cannot, indeed, be too emphatically urged that what is variously called moral principle, the law-abiding instinct, or conscience, is largely the result of constitutional causes over which we have no control—a physical condition, which may be inherited in a more or less perfect degree."

Nordau argued similarly (1900:259): "Morality—not that learnt mechanically, but that which we feel as an internal necessity—has become, in the course of thousands of generations, an organized instinct. For this reason, like all other organized instincts, it is exposed to 'perversion,' to aberration."

7. In addition to the typical degeneracy statements such as Lombroso's (1891), Nordau's (1900), and Babcock's (1895), this position is most clearly enunciated in Moreau (1859), Schilling (1866), Hagen (1877), Radestock (1884), Maudsley (1886), MacDonald (1892), Nisbet (1912), Schwarz (1916), and Kretschmer (1931).

8. In a statement of concession, Moreau (1859:499) granted the genius a limited degree of freedom that, however, can only serve to activate the intellectual "machinery": "Will seems to serve only to start the machinery thinking, so to speak, to make suitable use of the machinery, to facilitate its movement."

9. Translated by Anne McGovern.

10. A clarification is in order. While Moreau's is typical of the type of explanation that stresses the physico-chemical sources of the genius' basic lack of self-determinism, not all similar sources saw the degree of victimization as so nearly total. To Radestock, for instance, the genius is in possession of a constitutionally weak faculty of will. As such, Radestock believed that the genius is capable, in most cases, of strengthening his underdeveloped power of will and, in this way, of helping reduce the chance for mental disorder (Radestock, 1884:45,52).

11. Freud, it should be remembered, believed that successful sublimation enables the genius to escape an otherwise inevitable fate of mental disorder.

12. The degree to which the spokesmen for the pathology position subscribed to the Romantic interpretation of genius is interesting to observe. Moreau, for one, while judging the genius' absence of will as the result of a morbid nervous affliction, believed, nevertheless, that the intellectual accomplishments of the highest order were always the products of impulsive dictates of mind. "And (to recall it here in passing) the work is never better," he observed, "than . . . when it is accomplished without the direct participation of the will, almost unknown to the ego" (1859:495).

13. Of the fifteen cases in this sample that adopt a pro-sanity position on genius, only Padovan (1902) presents an exception to this rule. On the one hand, he stresses the observation that the genius is neurologically a totally healthy and "complete organization" (1902:305), yet describes the process of creation in characteristically Romantic terms. Describing his own condition during the time of writing his monograph on genius, Padovan provides this interesting account: "One by one, these Titans have become familiar to me; I feel the glory of their intelligence, I am burning and vibrating with enthusiasm. . . . So great is the fervour with which I have pursued my researches, so intense have been the suggestions emanating from the spiritual contact which I owe to them, that they have resulted in hallucinations; sometimes, when I stayed my pen for an instant, searching for a word, some of these men have appeared to me as though my spirit had summoned them (1902:2).

14. Of the monographs surveyed for this study, the pathology:health ratio for this period was 1.9 to 1.

Modern "Scientific" Models in the Genius-Madness Controversy

The association of genius with clinical insanity became firmly established as a scientific fact during the second half of the nineteenth century. The shift from the prevailing Enlightenment conception of the extraordinary creative individual as balanced and sane to the assessment of pathology was made possible, it has been seen, by modifications in a number of cultural axioms that pertained to the nature of man, the dynamics of original productivity, and the functioning of the mind. It has been argued that the men of genius, particularly those identified with the Romantic Movement, were frequently the major spokesmen for these intellectual changes and, trapped by their own sense of logic, proceeded to suggest that madness was a likely if not inevitable result of their condition.

But while the men of genius contributed to their own characterization as eccentric, moody, and mad, a number of intellectual developments particular to the nineteenth century served to foster a more clearly "scientific" and medical verdict of insanity. These developments, produced outside of those areas that since the Romantic period were defined as the foremost domain of genius—the realms of literature, the arts, and philosophic speculation—were contributions of a more scientific nature and were assigned the distinction of scientific "insight," "principle," or "law." And, while those who argued the case for the genius-madness association generally embraced the Romantic premises regarding genius and original creativity and, from these, derived the conclusion of madness, this by itself was not sufficient to elevate the discussion beyond the realm of "abstract" and "superficial" speculation. The notion of the abnormality of genius had been a subject of concern since the start of the Romantic Movement but lacked, prior to the mid-nineteenth century, the support of the scientific and, specifically, the medical community. The mid-nineteenth century, however, marked a growing participation on this issue by large numbers of the medical professions, and their position on the genius-madness controversy carried with it the weight of "science."[1] Unlike the former "authorities" on the issue, primarily the men of genius themselves, who commented with frequent incoherence on the conditions of their own health, the physician-psychiatrists of the nineteenth and twentieth centuries brought to bear the "latest" scientific tools and insights and talked with the authority of those who possessed a "license" to assess the mental health of others.[2]

The self-labeling by the Romantic men of genius was the result of their own musing on their own fates, and ended in a kind of self-condemnation. In the latter half of the nineteenth century, however, this condemnation was supported by a weight of "scientific" evidence, for the labelers were, overwhelmingly, the scientists themselves. And the new scientific insights or theories now applied to the association of genius and madness were rooted in a predominantly deterministic framework and, in that sense, tended to impose an aura of inevitability on the condition of genius. An examination of these "scientific" insights and models is next in order for this study.

THE CONCEPTION OF THE "AVERAGE MAN" IN THE CONTEXT OF EVOLUTIONARY THEORY

The distinction between genius and talent, introduced during the mid-eighteenth century and sharpened during the Romantic era, was principally intended, in the period preceding the madness controversy, to accentuate the extraordinary character of the man who was capable of the highest forms of original creativity. Unlike the man of talent, who differed from the ordinary man merely in quantitative terms or in the degree of mental acuity, the man of genius was unique in the sense that he was qualitatively set apart from the rest of humanity—it was a certain mysterious and largely indefinable qualitative difference in the genius that enabled him to experience the "unusual" states of mind (generally expressed in terms of "mania" and "divine inspiration") deemed essential for profound creativity. During the nineteenth and twentieth centuries, it has been seen, the sharp delineation of genius and talent was not endorsed by all participants engaged in the madness controversy. The spokesmen for the sanity of genius, intent on stressing the essential normalcy and naturalness of the mental processes of genius, rejected the sharp separation between the two and proceeded to define genius as more or less synonymous with talent, ability, intellect, intelligence, and "the gifted." Those who maintained the pathology position, on the other hand, overwhelmingly accepted the separation of genius and talent as a demonstrable fact.[3] But unlike the Romantics, who regarded this separation as evidence for the genius' magical and mysterious origin and his peculiar relation to the divine, the spokesmen for the pathology position assessed this distinction primarily in the context of insanity and ill health.

The classification of genius and talent as respectively disposed to pathology and sanity derived support from an intellectual development of the nineteenth century—the popularization of a mathematical or statistical conception of the average or normal man. Unlike the Romantic Period, when the "mere" man of talent was a common subject of derision and scorn, in the typical pro-pathology statements of the nineteenth and twentieth centuries, the status of the man of talent was that of an exceptional individual who, unlike the man of genius, was a typically stable, balanced, and healthy examplar of a normal man. The man of talent did not, however, based on his merits as a particularly skilled synthesizer of existing knowledge, become commonly hailed as a new and superior model for man.[4] His distinction was to be an exceptional representative of the normal or average man—and, to many, in the evolutionary vision of the nineteenth century, it was this average man who most maximized the chances for human survival and genuine progress.

The concept of the average or normal man derived its appeal during the nineteenth century from a variety of sources. We will be interested specifically in the development of the statistical conception of this "average" man, for it is this phenomenon that is most frequently encountered in the literature of the genius controversy, and one that conveniently lent itself to integration into a generally deterministic and evolutionary framework.[5] The more purely mathematical conceptualization of the average man is traceable to Adolphe Quételet and the development of the science of statistics during the 1840s.[6]

Based on his measurements of the physical characteristics of man, and particularly the heights and weights of individuals, Quételet advanced the idea of the "homme moyen," or the average man. Because he found his observations to be always symmetrically distributed about a mean or an average value—in a pattern anticipated from the binominal and normal (Gaussian) distributions—he proposed that the means of various traits be combined to establish one paradigmatic human being. This individual would represent the average "type" for a city, a nation, and even for all of humanity and, in that sense, constitutes a "type for human beauty" or a "type for physical perfection" (in Landau and Lazarsfeld: 254). To account for the fact that individual values consistently "oscillate," or tend to group themselves symmetrically around a mean "type" or "standard," he stipulated the existence of a general "law of accidental causes." And, while Quételet appeared unable to specify, concretely, the workings of this law and suggested that its operation is fortuitous in nature, he maintained that the variations around the mean are produced or "regulated" by this law "with such harmony and precision that we can classify them in advance numerically and by order of magnitude, within their limits" (in Landau and Lazarsfeld: 252). Moreover, Quételet was convinced, the "law of accidental causes" governs not only the physical traits of man, thus forming the basis for what he called "social physics," but presides over all moral and intellectual qualities as well and, therefore, establishes a scientific foundation for the study of "moral statics" (Landau and Lazarsfeld: 251).

Quételet's conceptualization of the "homme moyen" became, during the nineteenth century, the subject of a "most vigorous and widespread debate" among statisticians, philosophers, and social scientists (Landau and Lazarsfeld: 254).[7] Not surprisingly, the notion of the average man found entry into the controversy over the relationship of genius and madness. Those who argued the pathological condition of genius readily found support for their deterministic world views in Quételet's highly deterministic explanation of physical, intellectual, and moral regularities. The direction that the application of the average man to a deterministic assessment of genius was to take is manifestly apparent from

Galton's *Hereditary Genius,* first published in 1869 (see Galton, 1962).
In a discussion of his theoretical position, described in terms of the
law of "deviation from an average," Galton freely acknowledged
Quételet's pioneer contributions and believed his position to be consistent with that of his predecessor:

> Now, if this be the case with stature [distributed in a population
> according to the normal curve of distribution], then it will be
> true as regards every other physical feature—as circumference of
> head, size of brain, weight of grey matter, number of brain fibers,
> etc.; and thence, by a step on which no physiologist will hesitate,
> as regards mental capacity.

> This is what I am driving at—the analogy clearly shows there must
> be a fairly constant average mental capacity in the inhabitants of
> the British Isles, and that the deviations from that average—up-
> wards towards genius, and downwards towards stupidity—must
> follow the law that governs deviations from all true averages.
> [Galton:72] [8]

In 1892, in the preface to the reprint of the 1869 edition, Galton expounded on his application of the law of "deviation from an average"
(now called the law of the "frequency of errors") in an importantly
different way:

> Its application [the law of the frequency of error] had been ex-
> tended by Quételet to the proportions of the human body, on
> the grounds that the differences, say in stature, between men of
> the same race might theoretically be treated as if they were Errors
> made by Nature in her attempt to mold individual men of the
> same race according to the same ideal pattern. [Galton:28] [9]

To Galton, then, the variations distributed around a mean are interpreted, by 1892, in the context of some grand design or blueprint of
"Nature" and, in fact, it is the "Errors" of "Nature" that constitute
deviations from some "ideal pattern." But, while Galton suggested that
the average type is in some ways "preferred" and figures centrally in
the larger scheme of nature, this observation appears inconsistent with
his overall eugenic position: indeed, Galton had proposed (in 1869)
that it would be practicable to produce a highly gifted race of men by
judicious control of marriages for several successive generations. [10]
This paradox of, at one time, implying the desirability of breeding a
strain of geniuses and, later, of seeing nature's "average" as the closest

to perfection, can possibly be viewed as an accommodation to the pre-vailing temper of the times. If the intent were accommodation, however, it was not sufficient to deter printed criticism of his earlier position that eugenic control was feasible and, by implication, desirable if it would produce a strain of superior men. Few shared his position.[11] "It is bold conceit," observed Maudsley (1908:90), in a direct attack on Galton, "that man can yet interfere successfully in the complicated business and prescribe strict rules of good breeding whereby the genius shall be reproduced generation after generation, and the anti-social being eliminated from the social economy."

Even if the possibility of "raising" intellectually superior men were granted, there still remained the question of its "morality." As Lange-Eichbaum observed (1935:347):

> The idea of raising "geniuses" smatters not only of absurdity, but testifies to extraordinary cruelty. To be destined to become a man of genius means to be subjected, in the majority of cases and in accordance with theoretical principles, to a life of intense and gruesome martyrdom. The promotion of genius would, there-fore, be most inhumane.[12]

Far more important than the charge of cruelty, however, was the belief that the promotion of genius constitutes an "artificial" inter-ference in nature and evolutionary processes and would, therefore, prove detrimental to the survival of the human species. The obser-vation that the genius is always an exception and never more than a small minority meant to many, when placed in the evolutionary context of human survival, that nature did not intend the genius to become a dominant type. In his stead, it was the average man, or the type most frequently encountered, that appeared "favored" by nature. What insured the domination of the stable and healthy average man was that he, unlike all deviations from this type, was naturally prolific. As Maudsley (1908) observed:

> Not wholly unwarranted was the old saying, for it was the shrewd inference of common observation, that giants in the mind, like giants in the body, are commonly infertile. Nature, mindful of the species, careless of the single life, seems bent on a constant reversion to the average.[67]

> Even the sane genius [a rarity to Maudsley] is not granted the privilege of propagation and continuance of its exceptional self;

the rule of a steady return to the mean, enforcing a distribution of the accumulated capital, checks that hurt to the equilibrium of the species.[80]

In summary, then, even if it were possible to create a strain of geniuses by eugenic control, this promotion of the "errors of nature" would be cruel, unnatural, and, therefore, intensely undesirable.

Once defined as a variation from a normal or average type and, in that sense, regarded as less "favored" by nature, it was but a short step to the labeling of all geniuses as members of a "morbid" or "degenerate" group. To Maudsley, it has been seen, even the few healthy and sane men of genius are incapable of propagating their kind. This is inevitably so, he believed, since even the sane man of genius is derived from essentially pathological stock. "The great man does not make himself," observed Maudsley (1886:657), for "he needs and uses up the silently accumulated capital of generations of the family stock; the natural result after him, therefore, is commonly mediocrity or degeneracy." And, because the sane man of genius derives his health and intellectual vitality at the expense of his ancestors, his living relatives, and his descendants, there is, insisted Maudsley, "hardly ever a man of genius who has not insanity or nervous disorder of some form in his family" (1996:655). The sane genius, while himself not pathological or degenerate per se, possesses, as a member of a "morbid" group, aberrations and peculiarities that nature deems fit for extinction. As Nordau (1900:16) concurred, the "morbid deviation from an original type"—defined as gaps in development, malformations and infirmities—"does not continuously subsist and propagate itself, but, fortunately, is soon rendered sterile, and after a few generations often dies out." According to Nisbet (1912:317), this is fortunate indeed: "Had the human race consisted three hundred years ago of Shakespeares, Miltons, and Cromwells, it would long since have disappeared from the face of the earth."[13]

The recognition, during the nineteenth century in particular, of a statistically normal and average man, who was rigidly defined as the model of health and sanity, was tantamount to a narrowing of the boundaries of mental sanity. Not only the intellectually less gifted, but every mind whose capacity greatly surpassed the average or manifested extraordinary characteristics was labeled, accordingly, as diseased. W. Hirsch (1897), for one, perceived clearly the implications of the normal man concept and cautioned his professional peers: "As I have repeatedly remarked, psychology must strictly individualize; and I can imagine nothing more preposterous or unscientific than to assume a so-called normal man, and to conclude that anything which departs from that norm is diseased" (1897:73). With regard to the man of genius, Hirsch added, "No doubt, if we are to assume that whatever does not conform to the norm is to be considered as diseased, every man mentally famous must be set down, without further parley, as a pathological subject," (1897:73).[14] The "abuses" that Hirsch felt compelled to correct are perhaps best illustrated by a statement of justification provided by Nisbet (1912):

> It has been objected to my theory that neuropathy exists among the 'dolts and dunderheads' of the world in perhaps as great a degree as among the man of genius. Indeed, I should expect this to be the case wherever the dolts and dunderheads fall as much below the average level of mental capacity as men of genius rise above it. I expressly say that the soundest man is he who most nearly approaches the average. It is upon the medium type that Nature evidently relies for the continuance of the species, not upon extremes or accidental variation.[xxii]

> And it is worthy of remark that, as a rule, in their case [geniuses] the greater the genius the greater the unsoundness.[xxiv]

Nisbet's position, while providing a more rigid delineation of the average man from the genius than most, conveys, nevertheless, the general inclination characteristic of those who subscribed to the pathology verdict on genius. Most of his contemporaries who wrote on the controversy were, like him, prone to use the concept of the statistical average as the yardstick against which genius—and, concomittantly, madness—was judged. In this context, it is the man of talent who is most commonly treated as the foremost representative of this average type. This sane and healthy man of talent, observed Babcock (1895), constitutes the "highest type of our present state of evolution and civilization" (1895:749-750). And unlike his morbid and "degenerate cousin," the genius, the talented man's heritage "bespeaks a normal ancestry and his symmetry of physical contour a healthy organism" (1895:750).

MEN OF GENIUS AND
COLLECTIVE PSYCHOPATHOLOGY

The recognition of a statistically normal or average man who is strictly defined as a model of mental health and stability produced a situation where entire categories of people—all those who departed from the mean type—became subject to being classified as mentally ill. This narrowing of the boundaries of sanity, which has been seen to facilitate the typing of the genius as pathological, was further promoted by an intellectual development of the nineteenth century— the formulation of cultural and historical models of psychic epidemics.

The observation that the political and social environment has a direct impact on the physical and mental health of populations found general acceptance during the eighteenth century. In the intellectual climate of the Enlightenment—characterized by the central ideas of Design, Natural Law, Reason, and Happiness—there developed the basic assumption that the world was created in accordance with a definite plan. The degree to which man's institutions were in compliance with this orderly plan, described generally in terms of the laws of nature, indicated the potential for human happiness and health. To Benjamin Rush, a foremost exponent of Enlightenment thought in America, the conditions for maximum mental and physical health were to be found in an agricultural setting exemplified by the young American Republic (Rosen, 1969:177). Based on his examination of the fluctuations of various types (some newly identified) of mental illness for the periods preceding, during, and following the American Revolutionary War, Rush concluded that political and economic institutions are so intimately related to mental and physical disease that any acute social change has to lead, inevitably, to accompanying changes in the general health of the population.[15] Following Rush, comparable studies for the French Revolution of 1789 (Pinel and Petit), the revolutions of 1848-1849 (de Boimont and Virchow), and the Franco-Prussian War (Hospital) confirmed the observation that greatly disruptive phenomena, such as wars and revolutions, stimulate increases in various types of mental disorder (see Rosen: 178-182). The interest created by these and similar examinations led to a continued and widespread study of the connection between sociopolitical change and mental disturbances, and culminated, around the middle of the nineteenth century, in the creation of various theories of epidemic disease. Best articulated and most famous of these is a theory developed by the physician Rudolph Virchow in conjunction with his co-workers Leubuscher and Neumann (see Rosen:179).

Reasoning by analogy, Virchow established a parallel between the individual and larger society. "If disease is an expression of individual life under unfavourable conditions," he observed, "the epidemics must be indicative of major disturbances of mass life" (in Rosen:195). These upheavals are in the nature of not only "atmospheric" and "cosmic" changes, but, more significant for mankind, include those that are political, economic, and cultural in origin. Differentiating between "natural" and "artificial" epidemics, a distinction based on the degree to which cultural factors are interposed between nature and man, Virchow proposed that "artificial" epidemics appear at nodal points in history, the periods marked by intellectual revolution, social contradictions, economic changes, and political turmoil:

> The history of artificial epidemics is therefore the history of disturbances which the civilization of mankind has experienced. Its changes show us with powerful strokes the turning points at which civilization moves off in new directions. Every true cultural revolution is followed by epidemics because a large part of the people only gradually enter into the new cultural movement and begin to enjoy its blessings. [in Rosen:180]

Included in Virchow's sociohistorical theory of epidemic disease is the phenomenon identified as psychic epidemics. He observed that:

> The artificial epidemics are physical or mental, for mental diseases also occur epidemically and tear entire peoples into a mad psychotic movement. Psychiatry alone enables the historian to survey and understand the major fluctuations of public opinion and popular feeling, which on the whole resemble the picture of individual mental illness. [in Rosen:180]

In an application of this type of argument to the psychological reactions observed by himself and others during the revolutionary activities in 1848, Virchow concluded that the rise in mental disturbance was, in fact, a widespread psychic epidemic caused by man's interference in natural historical processes (in Rosen:181).

Closely related to the more purely sociohistorical theories of epidemic disease, of which Virchow's is a foremost example, is a large body of literature produced during the nineteenth and twentieth centuries that addressed, in more general terms, the question of mental illness in its relationship to modern civilization. Similar to Virchow and the other investigators of political, economic, and religious upheavals who endeavored to understand the occurrences of psychic epidemics in terms of collective psychopathology, those who explored the connection between civilization and mental disease advanced the idea that entire portions of the population are mentally ill and deserve to be seen as products of widely prevalent pathology-spawning conditions in the sociocultural realm. While these contributors to the madness-civilization literature are distinguishable by their relative emphasis on various factors held to be productive of illness, a common theme nevertheless is discernible and centers on the "evils" of modern-urban-industrial society. As George Burrows observed in 1828:

> Many of the causes inducing intellectual derangement, and which are called moral, have their origin not in individual passions or feelings, but in the state of society at large; and the more artificial, i.e. civilized society is, the more do these causes multiply and extensively operate. [in Rosen:183]

In 1852, Edward Jarvis, expounding on the dangers of complex and mechanical civilization, wrote:

> Insanity is then a part of the price we pay for civilization. The causes of the one increase with the developments and results of the other.... [With civilization] come more opportunities and rewards for great and excessive mental action, more uncertain and hazardous employments, and consequently more disappointments, more means of provocations for sensual indulgence, more dangers of accidents and injuries, more groundless hopes, and more painful struggle to obtain that which is beyond reach, or to effect that which is impossible. [in Rosen, 186-187]

And while a few individuals during the nineteenth century questioned the assertion that civilization is intimately related to insanity,[16] the idea of the baneful effects of modern society were generally accepted on faith, despite the fact that the statistical evidence was, at best, of most dubious validity.[17] Jarvis spoke, therefore, with the weight of consensus when he concluded: "The deductions, then, drawn from the prevalence and effects of causes, corroborate the opinion of nearly all writers, whether founded on positive and known facts, on analogy, on computations or on conjuncture, that insanity is an increasing disease. In this opinion all agree" (in Rosen:187).

The persistence of the view that insanity increases with the degree of societal complexity led, in the second half of the nineteenth and in the first half of the twentieth centuries, to the question of differential prevalence. This concern with the distribution of madness was centered on all conceivable groups and populations ranging from comparisons among the sexes (e.g., E. Sheppard, 1873), races (e.g., J. B. Andrews, 1887), and cultures (e.g., D. G. Brinton, 1902) to those of social class (e.g., Hellpach, 1906) and the degree of intellectual attainment (e.g., D. H. Tuke, 1878).[18] And, indeed, the literature comprising the genius-madness controversy deserves to be seen, most generally, as a contribution to this larger concern. The issue of genius and insantiy, discussed often in the larger contexts of social class, education, and intelligence, proceeded from the general assumption—one that was consistent with the "average man" concept—that the "upper" and "lower" fringes of society are most susceptible to madness. Daniel Hack Tuke reflected this assumption (1878:94):

> Alternately swayed by the evidence which presents itself, now in the higher, now in the lower ranks of society, of the fearful consequences of certain lines of conduct and living alike ending in insanity, we seem at one time driven to the conclusion that a refined and overcivilized life, and at another that an unlettered one, most favours the spread of mental disorder. The right conclusion is, however, that both present their peculiar perils in different forms.

Concerning the genius in particular, the sociocultural "perils" that spawned insanity were commonly assessed as twofold in origin. Not only was he exposed, like most other men, to the ill-effects of rapid social change and modernization, but he was subject as well to the unique hazards of a more "refined" and "lettered" way of life. It is in this context of disenchantment and despair with modern civilized life, then, that the issue of the insanity of genius was explored during the nineteenth century. Goethe, a voice of cultural malaise in the days preceding the "scientific" accounts of genius and madness, observed in 1828 that a scholarly existence is particularly susceptible to the baneful effects of modernization. Unlike the natural and healthy lifestyle of the peasantry, the intellect—almost always "tied to his desk" and inclined to a more "artificial" and "complicated" existence—was seen to have incurred a general weakening to his constitution and was thought to suffer from the "demon of hypochondria" (see Möbius, 1909:155-158). And as a possessor of an inordinate degree of sensitivity and an ideal vision of the future, it is this individual, in this view, who is inclined to perceptions of social maladjustments and cultural contradictions. Given the delicateness of the intellect's constitution, observed Goethe, the perception of social tensions and instabilities results in frustrations and disappointments that may lead, in turn, to a deterioration in the intellect's mental and physical condition (in Möbius:159-160). Commenting on the future health of German society, Goethe expressed the hope that it should be blessed not with "abstract scholars and philosophers," but with "ordinary humans" ("Menschen") in their stead (in Möbius:158).

Goethe's observations, however, while positing a connection between the sociocultural environment and mental disturbance in the genius, were nevertheless cautious and premonitory. The proposed relationship was neither systematically developed nor specifically tied to concrete individuals, and it was concerned not with the more serious forms of mental illness, but with what he perceived as the neurasthenia or nervous debility ("Nervenschwäche") that afflicted virtually all members of the population.[19] For the more systematically "thought through" explanations of the relation of the sociocultural realm to insanity in the extraordinary man, one has to turn to the mad genius literature proper and, specifically, to those works that argued on behalf of the pathological condition of genius.[20] Although it is not practicable to present the views of every writer on the subject—the major differences consisting of the relative stress each placed on a number of commonly identified variables and the differing methods proposed to ameliorate the debilitating effects—at least one work can not be omitted from this discussion. Max Nordau's *Degeneration* constitutes what is unquestionably the most controversial treatment of the relation of the sociocultural environment to mental and physical aberration. First published in 1892 under the title of *Entartung* and translated into English in 1895, it raised such an immediate storm of controversy that by 1900 it had gone through nine English-speaking editions. Indeed, an entire literature developed over *Degeneration*, one that includes George Bernard Shaw's famous rebuttal, *The Sanity of Art* (1895).[21]

Applying Morel's and Lombroso's conceptualization of "degeneracy" to the originators of the new aesthetic and literary tendencies, Nordau predicted the coming of a human catastrophe of unprecedented proportions for the Western World. He believed the works of most contemporary greats such as Schopenhauer, Nietzsche, Tolstoy, Ibsen, Wagner, Zola, and such popular phenomena as realism, naturalism, symbolism, and mysticism to be symptomatic of the twin evils of the age—"degeneration" and "hysteria." "We stand now in the midst of a severe mental epidemic," he proclaimed (Nordau:537), "of a sort of black death of degeneration and hysteria."[22] While these twin maladies have always taken their toll among mankind, observed Nordau, they have shown themselves only sporadically in the days preceding the Industrial Revolution and were consequently of minor importance to the total health of the pre-industrial community. Pointedly, continues the author (Nordau:43), it is the "excessive organic wear and tear" and "fatigue" produced by the modern industrial society that has raised the frequency of degeneration and hysteria to epidemic proportions. Specifically, with regard to the state of degeneracy in England, Nordau observed (1900:75):

> Trade, industry, and civilization were nowhere in the world so much developed as in England. Nowhere did men work so assiduously, nowhere did they live under such artificial conditions as these. Hence the state of degeneration and exhaustion, which we observe today in all civilized countries as the result of this overexertion, must of necessity have shown itself sooner in England than elsewhere, and, as a matter of fact, did show itself in the third and fourth decade of the century with continually increasing violence.[23]

Distinguishing between degeneracy and hysteria, Nordau regarded the former as a far more debilitating condition that proved particularly dangerous to the social order. Defined as a progressive state of biological and mental deterioration and constituting a reversion from a "higher" to a less complex organism, degeneracy is recognizable by concrete physical and intellectual "stigmata" or "brand-marks." What accounts for the progressive nature of degeneracy, to Nordau, is its dependency on sociocultural and hereditary processes. While traceable to "unfavourable influences" such as residency in large towns, political and social upheavals, adulterated foods, the intake of alcohol, tobacco, coffee, and such similar products (Nordau:34-35), once degeneracy manifests itself in individuals it becomes genetically transmissible:

> When under any kind of noxious influences an organism becomes debilitated, its successors will not resemble the healthy, normal type of the species, with capacities for development, but will form a new subspecies, which, like all others, possesses the capacity of transmitting to its offspring, in a continuously increasing degree, its peculiarities, these being morbid deviations from the normal type—gaps in development, malformations and infirmities. [Nordau:16]

Fortunately for mankind, wrote Nordau, this morbid condition is "soon rendered sterile, and after a few generations often dies out before it reaches the lowest grade of organic degradation" (Nordau:16).

While to Nordau the term degeneracy is in reference to an entire "anthropological family"—one that includes not only authors and artists, but also criminals, prostitutes, anarchists, and pronounced lunatics—his sense of alarm is clearly reserved for those contemporary individuals of extraordinary prominence who satisfy their "unhealthy impulses" in the areas of literature, philosophy, music, and painting (Nordau:vii). It is this group of "graphomaniacs," "mattoids," "borderland dwellers," and "dégénérés supérieurs" that is responsible for the coming crisis in Western society.[24] As members of a degenerate stock, the works of the "higher degenerates" always bespeak their identity as "anti-social vermin"; their products reflect the mental "stigmata" of all degenerates—a decrease in morality, an unbridled egoism, impulsiveness, pessimism, emotionalism, and a pronounced enthusiasm for morbidly mystical and religious concerns (Nordau:18-22).

The works of degenerate authors and artists, however, are not harmful per se, observed Nordau. The danger presents itself in the existence of growing numbers of enthusiastic followers who proclaim these works as "the guides to the promised land of the future" (Nordau:25). Indeed, he reasoned, it is a misfortune for Western society that increasing numbers have lost their natural ability to distinguish the depraved and degenerate products from those that are healthy and sane. It is this rising inability among the general population to discern what is worthy that has produced in the late nineteenth century an intellectual climate—characterized by the term "fin de siècle"—characterized by escapism, world-weariness, and decadence in art and literature. The "fin de siècle" characteristics are prima facie harmful to the social fabric, wrote Nordau, because they include, among others, an "emancipation from traditional discipline," an "unbridled lewdness," "the unchaining of the beast in man," "the trampling under foot of all barriers which enclose brutal greed of lucre and lust of pleasure," the "repudiation of dogma," and the "vanishing of ideals in art" (Nordau: 5).

Like the "higher degenerates"—those who are the producers of modern literature and art—their devoted followers are judged by Nordau as similarly diseased. The latter, however, are not degenerates but victims of "hysteria," a condition akin to neurasthenia that has its origin in the growth of large towns and the general "fatigue of the present generation" (Nordau:36).[25] The leading characteristic of the hysterical persons—and it is this that makes them a danger to society— is their "disproportionate" tendency to yield to suggestion (Nordau: 25). A consequence of this susceptibility to suggestion in the hysterical subject, observed Nordau, is his irresistible passion for imitation: "When he sees a picture, he wants to become like it in attitude and dress; when he reads a book, he adopts its views blindly" (Nordau: 26). It is the impressionability of the hysterical individual, cautioned Nordau, that has led, particularly in the case of Germany, to the popular expression of anti-Semitism (Nordau:209). What makes both the degenerates and hysterics dangerous to the social fabric is that they, like criminals, "unite in bands" in order to pursue their "perverse" interests more effectively. In the realm of literature and the arts it is this characteristic that leads to "the formation of close groups or schools uncompromisingly exclusive to outsiders" (Nordau:29). The joining of degenerates and hysterics in the formation of sects, bands, artistic circles, and schools of thought is inevitable, observed Nordau, because "persons of highly-strung nerves attract each other" (Nordau: 30).

In Nordau's judgment, however, this alarming situation in the Western World, is not totally beyond amelioration. Much could be done to "reduce the disease of the age 'to its anatomical necessity'" (Nordau:551) and it is to this end, he urged, that every effort must be directed. It is evident that those "higher degenerates" whose mental derangement is too deep-seated "must be abandoned to their inexorable fate. . . . They will rave for a season, and then perish" (Nordau:551). But in addition to those who are irrevocably the victims of their organic constitution, the contemporary artistic and intellectual tendencies are pursued and promoted by the large number of hysterical victims. We can and must save the majority of this group of "misguided" individuals from the "cunning impostures," the "higher degenerates." The failure to comply with this warning, cautioned Nordau, would inevitably result in a further escalation of the epidemic of hysteria. If society continues the practice of passively abandoning hysterical subjects to the influences of "graphomaniacal fools" and their "imbecile or unscrupulous bodyguard of critics," wrote Nordau:

> The inevitable result of such neglect of duty would be a much more rapid and violent outspread of the mental contagion, and civilized humanity would with much greater difficulty, and much more slowly, recover from the mental contagion disease of the age than it might under strong and resolute combat with the evil. [Nordau:551-552]

The reduction in the virulence of hysteria, and to a lesser degree degeneracy, is possible, predicted Nordau, only through the forced removal of all "degenerate" ideas and tendencies from public circulation (Nordau:558-560). It is towards this goal that all "healthy and moral men" must strive and act with immediacy, for the time lost in indecision and settling on a "best" course of action means that the progressive "poisoning" of an entire generation is allowed to continue unchecked (Nordau:557).

To Nordau, then, and this characteristic is shared by most of those who endorsed a pro-pathology position on genius, the phenomenon of mental illness must be treated not as a problem of individualized afflictions, but under the rubric of collective psychopathology.[26] The belief, commonly endorsed during much of the nineteenth and twentieth centuries, that insanity is intimately related to modern civilization and tied to political, economic, and intellectual upheavals, led to the assumption that mental disturbance is a prevalent and generally increasing phenomenon to which particular groups of people are especially susceptible. The men of genius—generally defined as constituting a singularly uniform category of man with such inherently collective attributes as a "delicate constitution," a melancholic temperament, a limited power of will, and a dangerously dominant imagination—were seen as most unlikely to withstand the strains and tensions of modern society. It is not surprising, therefore, that a clear majority of those who addressed the question of genius and madness endorsed the verdict that the condition of genius constitutes a form of pathology; in their judgments, the exemplars of totally sane or healthy geniuses were either few or totally nonexistent. In the case of Nordau, the sane men of genius are seen overwhelmingly as a blessing of the past; the vast majority of the contemporary "greats" are viewed as the unfortunate and dangerous products of the ongoing process of modernization and the epidemic-like spread of degeneracy.[27] Finally, the charge of collective psychopathology was not unique in its application to the men of genius. It was commonly applied to other types of degenerates—the criminals, prostitutes, anarchists, and lunatics—and, with Nordau, to the enthusiastic admirers of the "higher degenerates"—the hysterics. In fact, the majority of contemporary "greats," themselves victims of "contagious" influences and collective pathology, were believed to contribute to the escalation of yet another epidemic disease—hysteria.

Thus the narrowing definitions of sanity, and the identification of modern industrial society as a fertile and expanding spawning ground for mental illness, made almost inevitable the conviction of collective pathology. Among the groups encompassed by this rubric, it was also almost inevitable, given previous assessments, that the men of genius would be prominently included. And they were, not only as victims of collective pathology, but as catalytic elements as well.

NOTES

1. It should be recalled that of the 46 individuals in this study's sample who addressed the pathology question and for whom information indicating professional affiliation has been located, 26 were found to have earned a degree in medicine. Of these, all but four were seen to endorse a pro-pathology argument. And while a substantial number who wrote on the issue were not members of the medical professions, those commonly defined as the leading authorities on the question were, and included such persons as Moreau, Lombroso, Maudsley, Nordau, Lange-Eichbaum, and Kretschmer.

2. An interesting dilemma was presented by the fact that throughout the course of the mad genius debate the term genius was generally applied not only to distinguished individuals in the arts and letters, but to the "greats" in the more purely scientific disciplines as well. It was possible, therefore, that those who argued the pro-pathology case most eloquently would become subject to the distinction of genius and, by extension, the label of madness. Most commonly, the way one guarded against this situation, as a contributor to the dialogue, was to insist that the man of science, unlike the poet and artist, does not depend on a dominant imagination and, hence, derives protection from the powers of logical

criticism and judgment. On the other hand, in the classic degeneracy statement of Nordau, the situation is compounded by the insistence that the contemporary genius could hardly ever be sane; the healthy genius was defined as a blessing of the past. Nordau, in his dedication of his work to Lombroso, therefore, felt constrained to refer to his mentor not as a great genius, but as "one of the loftiest mental phenomena of the century" (Nordau, 1900:IX). Those like Schwarz (1916:388), who distinguished the basically sane "true geniuses from the pathological "quasi-genii," found it less difficult to extend the distinction of genius to a respected fellow contributor to the debate—one such as Nordau.

3. Lange-Eichbaum (1927, 1930) and Jaspers (1926), it will be recalled, are the two "exceptions" to endorse a pro-pathology verdict and, simultaneously, subscribe to a rational view of genius.

4. It appears, in fact, that those who sharply distinguished the man of talent from the genius share a considerable ambivalence for the former. It was difficult to exult in a man so clearly inferior and auxiliary to the genius—one defined as "mostly concerned with applying, interpreting, modifying, verifying . . . the creations of the genius" (Schwarz:11).

Lombroso commented critically on the envious "defamers" of genius, the men of talent:

> In this persecution, men of genius have no fiercer or more terrible enemies than the men of academies, who possess the weapons of talent, the stimulus of vanity, and the prestige by preference accorded to them by the vulgar, and by governments which, in large part, consist of the vulgar. [36]

> It is sufficient to be present at any academy, university, faculty, or gathering of men who, without genius, possess at least erudition, to perceive at once that their dominant thought is always disdain and hate of the man who possesses . . . the quality of genius. [62]

Lombroso, ironically, himself a lifelong "defamer" of genius, held a variety of academic appointments.

5. Among these sources, no doubt the advancement of a democratic ideology was prominent. The notion of the average person, when specifically traceable to a "democratic" bias of man, takes the general form of juxtaposing the ill-judgment and overall morbidity of the exceptional man to the "common good sense (and) the correct and healthy judgment of the masses" (see Moreau:494).

6. For an authoritative overview of Quételet's conception of the average man see Landau and Lazarsfeld, *International Encyclopedia Of The Social Sciences,* Vol. 13, 1968, 247-255.

7. Particularly controversial was Quételet's assertion that by combining the average nonphysical characteristics of men, a "type" would be constructed that represents most closely, an ideal of moral virtue and intellectual perfection. The most famous criticism of Quételet was provided in 1876 by Bertillon who argued that the construction of an average "type," especially in the area of intellect, would constitute a personification of mediocrity and the "type de la vulgarité" (see Landau and Lazarsfeld: 255).

8. Note: All quotations cited from Galton have been excerpted from the 1962 Meridian Book edition, which is a reprint of the 1892 and 1869 editions.

9. It is also interesting to note that, unlike the 1869 edition, Galton takes a position in the 1892 prefatory chapter on the issue of genius and madness. While rejecting the "extreme positions of Lombroso and others," Galton endorses a pathology verdict on genius:

> Still, there is a large residuum of evidence which points to a painfully close relation between the two [genius and madness], and I must add that my own later observations have tended in the same direction, for I have been surprised at finding how often insanity or idiocy has appeared among the near relatives of exceptionally able men. Those who are over eager and extremely active in mind must often possess brains that are more excitable and peculiar than is consistent with soundness. [Galton:27]

10. There is no evidence to suggest that Galton, in later years, wavered from this original eugenic position. He observed in 1892 that "The processes of evolution are in constant and spontaneous activity, some pushing towards the bad, some towards the good. Our part is to watch for opportunities to intervene by checking the former and giving free play to the latter" (Galton:41).

11. The most striking exception in this study's sample is N. Hirsch (1931) who, following Galton, proposed a three-fold program involving: (1) "positive eugenics," or increasing the number of individuals with high intelligence, (2) "negative eugenics," or decreasing the number of individuals with low intelligence, and (3) "Euthenics," which involves the creation of a social environment favorable to the promotion of genius. On the issues of madness and genius, Hirsch, while admitting to the greater susceptibility of the genius to neuroticism, suggests that the genius must be evaluated on his own grounds and not be compared to the average man. The "Genius is another psycho-biological species," he observed, "differing as much from man, in his mental and temperamental processes, as man differs from the ape" (1931:298).

A position similar to N. Hirsch is provided by Schwarz (1916), who believed the chances for moral and intellectual advancement to inhere not in the "average man" but the "true" and "many-sided" genius (1916:395). It is this "true" and "moral" genius, defined by Schwarz as the highest "kind of adaptation" (1916: 48), who is not to be confused with the "philistine" and "pseudo-superior man," a representative, in turn, of "morbid, exhausted, decadent, weak, despairing, insane [and] impotent" stock (1916:386).

12. Translated by this author.

13. Möbius (1909) provides a concrete example of this type of argument. Noting that Goethe's ancestors and descendents were of intellectually mediocre and physically diseased stock, he observed: "Goethe's family stock is devitalized; his family brought forth a precious blossom and in the process became drained of its vigor; after Goethe there followed only weak life impulses. The genius appears in the world not to increase the number of the human species—his works are his eternal descendents" (1909:263-264). (Translated by this author.)

14. It is curious to note that, while W. Hirsch insists on "individualization" in psychology, and defines all "true" geniuses as essentially healthy and sane, he distinguishes these geniuses, nevertheless, from those "partially gifted degenerates"

and "pseudo-geniuses" who, like the Realists and Naturalists, transgress artistic and intellectual conventions (135).

15. Rush, a co-signer of the Declaration of Independence, argued, for example, that opposition to the American Revolution constituted evidence of mental illness that he labeled "protection fever" or "Revolutiana." On the other hand, women who suffered from hysteria were, in Rush's view, cured of their condition through their support of the revolutionary cause. After the Peace of 1783, Rush observed that "The excess of the passion for liberty, inflamed by the successful issue of the war, produced, in many people, opinions and conduct which could not be removed by reason nor restrained by government" (in Szasz, 1970:140). Rush classified this "undesirable" conduct as a type of insanity, distinguished by the name of "Anarchia."

16. P. L. Panum provided a discrepant observation when he wrote in 1846:

> Since it has been proved that the frequency of mental diseases is generally in direct proportion to civilization and its accompanying social collisions, it might be surmised that these diseases are extremely rare on the Faroes, inasmuch as civilization has certainly not attained a high degree there, and the social collisions so agitating to the mind, under the patriarchal conditions which prevail, are proportionally very few. But on the contrary, there is hardly any other country or indeed any metropolis, in which mental diseases are so frequent in proportion to the number of people as the Faroes. [in Rosen:186]

17. Daniel Hack Tuke (1878:132-133, 136), for example, fully recognized that the registered increase in insanity for Britain during the last part of the nineteenth century was in large measure the consequence of improvements in the compilation of statistics as well as an expanded program of social legislation and Parliamentary concern for the detection and treatment of the insane. He chose, nevertheless, to admit the probability that insanity was on the rise:

> Whether, however, there is not also an actual increase, unaccounted for by population, or by accumulation, remains an open question, which statistics do not absolutely determine. At the same time I think that it is quite probable that there has been some real increase. [Tuke:89]

Indeed, this conclusion is the overall theme of Tuke's survey of madness in ancient and modern societies (see Tuke, 1878).

18. For a discussion of these contributions, excluding Tuke's, see Rosen:182-194.

19. In 1829, for example, he proposed the "hypothesis" that neurasthenia was a characteristic of the nineteenth century that, in the case of Germany, was caused by the attempt to gain political and intellectual independence from the French. This general weakening, he believed, afflicted not only painters, musicians, poets, sculptors, and natural scientists, but the "masses" as well (see Möbius:155).

20. It is not suggested that everyone in this study's sample who argued a propathology position on genius did so specifically in the context of the larger sociocultural environment. Those, for example, who approached the problem from a more purely psychological or psychoanalytical perspective, such as Stekel (1909,

1917), Hoffmann (1909), Sadger (1910), Hinkle (1923), and Baisch (1939), focused primarily on family tensions, sexual maladjustments, and overpowering libidinal energies. Others, like Radestock (1884) and Sanborn (1886), did not go beyond Goethe's observations to an appreciable degree, and were content to reiterate the idea that men of genius suffered debilitating, madness-producing effects from such factors as poverty, urban living, the addiction to alcoholism ("dipsomania"), opium, tobacco and coffee, the lack of appreciation, and so forth.

21. As recently as 1968, Nordau's work was republished in the United States (Encyclopaedia Judaica, 1971, Vol. 12: 1212) and, more than a half century after its first publication, it is found as a subject of doctoral dissertations: see, for example, M. P. Foster's *Reception of Max Nordau's "Degeneration" in England and America* (Ph.D. diss., Univ. of Michigan, 1954) and M. Gold's *Nordau on Degeneration: A Study of the Book and Its Cultural Significance* (Ph.D. diss., Columbia Univ., 1957).

22. Note: This and all the following quotations from Nordau are excerpted from the ninth D. Appleton and Company edition of 1900.

23. In the cases of France and Germany, Nordau perceived a similar situation. With regard to the former, we are told, the "upper ten thousands" are victims of degeneracy (Nordau:2), whereas recent events in Germany—rapid industrialization, urbanization and "two great wars"—have produced a situation where "we [the Germans] have very nearly overtaken the unenviable start which the English and French had over us in this direction" (Nordau:208).

24. These are terms that Nordau adopted from Lombroso ("mattoids" and "graphomaniacs"), Magnan ("dégénérés supérieurs"), and Maudsley and Ball ("borderland dwellers"). "Graphomania" is employed by Nordau (1900:17) to describe the impulsive quality of many degenerates to express and constantly repeat their "perverse" ideas in writing.

25. Nordau does not always distinguish sharply between degeneracy and hysteria. Generally, the latter is discussed as a condition akin to degeneracy that is, nevertheless, a milder affliction. Importantly, the hysterical person does not display the physical "stigmata" characteristic of the degenerate subject.

26. Exceptions are those individuals, like Hoffman (1909), Sadger (1910), and others, who examined the question of the sanity of genius from a more purely psychological or psychoanalytical perspective and focused on the particulars of child-rearing, sexual adjustment, and similar developmental "difficulties." Even with these, however, the assumption is made that men of genius as a category are victims of an unresolved "mother-complex" (Sadger), hereditary and chronic incapacities (Sadger, Hoffmann), or some other deficiency.

27. Indeed, it is interesting to observe that Nordau was most reluctant to apply the term genius to the "greats" of his age. Because he perceived so few of them to be totally sane, the distinction of the term "genius" was reserved for the extraordinary men of the past. His critics, however, consistently responded to his theories as condemnations of the genius class.

The Label of "Madness" and the Dynamic of Change 8

The "modern" conception of genius—as the manifestation of the highest degree of innate original ability in individuals—was popularized at the start of the eighteenth century and marks the culmination of an intermittent intellectual debate that had its beginnings with the Renaissance. The Italian humanists, under the spell of Graeco-Roman artistic and literary accomplishments, evolved the ideal of the "genio," a term reserved for those persons esteemed greatest in the arts and speculation who were believed to be the possessors of superior creative ability. To the men of the Renaissance, however, modern man was judged incapable of improving upon the works of the ancients; hence, "creativity" was conceived primarily in terms of the imitation of the established "masters" and of nature. Unlike the modern view of the genius that stresses "originality" as its distinguishing mark, the "genio" was described in terms of the "imitatio-ideal." It was not until about the mid-sixteenth century that an increasing number began to chafe under what, to them, appeared to be an excessive deference toward the masters of the past. Telesio, Vasari, Leonardo, and others challenged the "imitatio-ideal" and suggested that the "genio" should not be just imitatively creative, but newly creative as well. This attempt at redefinition, however, was generally rejected and remained a minority position for the remainder of the Renaissance. The rejection was ameliorated only in

107

cases such as the scientifically oriented literature, the engineer, and the inventor—men who were believed capable of building upon the achievements of the ancients and, in this sense, were encouraged to be newly creative. In the realm of arts and letters the "imitatio-ideal" prevailed; manifestations of originality generally had to be justified as eclectic, or as meeting the dictum of faithfulness to nature (Zilsel, 1926:247-255).[1]

The issue of imitation versus originality, after a relative period of calm, flared once again in 1687 with the famous "Quarrel of the Ancients and the Moderns." This controversy was triggered by Charles Perrault's reading of a poem ("Century of Louis the Great") before the French Academy in which he stressed the scientific superiority of the moderns and proclaimed the literary achievements of his day as superior to the works of Homer. The reaction was immediate. The greatest French writers of the time, Racine, LaFontaine, LaBruyère, and Boileau, conscious of their debt to the Greek and Roman classics, ardently defended the superiority of the ancients. It was Fontenelle who, a year following Perrault's reading of the poem, expounded a compromise position in an essay entitled "Digression on the Ancients and the Moderns." While he acknowledged, in support of Perrault, the possibility of infinite progress in the sciences, Fontenelle saw the potential for improvement in literature and the arts to be limited; unlike the sciences, the latter were subject not to "accurate reasoning" and the steady accumulation of knowledge, but depended primarily on the sharpness of the faculty of imagination, a faculty that could not be honed by education. Hence the moderns are not likely to surpass the most profound achievements of the ancients, reasoned Fontenelle, but must be content to strive and hope, at best, occasionally to equal the splendor of the ancient works (Havens, 1966: 83-86).[2]

Buttressed by the qualified approval of Fontenelle, Perrault's ideas did much to advance the cause of "originality" and "progress" in intellectual life. It is true that most, and particularly those engaged in literature and the arts, continued to remain subject to the authority of the academies and the traditional forms, but the restraints were no longer universally effective. Perrault's position in the "Quarrel of the Ancients and the Moderns" had fostered support as well as opposition, and one of the ways this support found expression was in an attempt to develop a new model of a superior man. It was the evolvement of the modern conception of genius during the eighteenth century that, perhaps more than any other single factor, was central to the eventual victory of the moderns, and made originality the definitive mark of all superior intellectual production. The definition of the genius as an innately gifted individual with an extraordinary capacity for imaginative creation, original thought, invention, and discovery, established him as the foremost enemy of tradition, imitation, and the conventional order. The genius, unlike the mere man of talent, could not be content with imitation and the synthesis of existing knowledge, but, driven by some mysterious and impulsive need, was compelled to express that which was original.[3] While in the earliest formulations on the nature of genius, as evidenced by Gerard, Duff, and others (see Fabian, 1966:IX-XLVIII), there was a tendency to define the creative and original impulse in genius as necessarily subject to the tempering influences of a piercing judgment, taste, and memory; the Romantics gradually disposed of the "rational" counterweights to the creative imagination and stressed the need for a near or total disregard for all authorities and traditional constraints in order to make possible profound, original creativity. It is the popularization of a more purely Romantic conceptualization of genius around the turn of the nineteenth century that constitutes perhaps the most complete triumph for the moderns in their struggle for originality and intellectual freedom.

The growing acceptance of the genius, however, as one who is impelled by his inmost nature to pursue the novel, was not without its perils to conventional society. This stress on originality—the foremost attribute of the truly great man—established the genius as the relentless destroyer of tradition and the enemy of conventional forms. In this sense, he could be seen as an agent of change and revolution. The Romantics, whether or not they were aware of the perils of this role, sought to legitimatize the prestige and power of the genius by suggesting that the extraordinary man was somehow destined to perform a sacred function. As a possessor of some essential "Urwahrheit" or primal truth, the genius was projected as a chosen "renovator" of the world or a guiding light of the age compelled to "improve" upon the works of God. And, as Carlyle proposed for the rest of humanity, its task was to recognize the genius as a law unto himself and enthusiastically engage in his veneration (see Zilsel, 1918:197).[4] The nature and function of the modern genius were becoming clearly defined.

The nineteenth century's fascination with heroes and the great-man theory and, more specifically, its ecstatic celebration of the newly creative man ("Originalgenie"), did much to establish the genius as a dominant force in history, a force potentially disruptive to conventionality and to established interests. Enhancing the power of those defined as geniuses were a number of historic developments: printing became less expensive, with the result that more people received the published work; literacy became more common, especially among the rising middle class; and women, particularly from the middle class, were on the way to becoming a responsive, literate group on their own. In short, the general consumption of art and the printed word grew enormously (Coser, 1970:6). And the development of mass democracy provided an atmosphere where those venerated by the public rode a high wave of prestige and power—popular support could transform the ideas of men of genius into historical events.

The question of the genius' power, and whether his inherent quest for originality and novel solutions is in conflict with what is best for men and society, constitutes a central concern of most monographs written on the genius-madness issue. Overwhelmingly, in fact, the very conclusion of sanity or madness is tied intimately to the particular position adopted on this question. For example, in his critical reply to Nordau's *Degeneration,* George Bernard Shaw sought to demonstrate the wholesomeness and sanity of modern artistic and literary expression, and proposed that the genius, far from being dangerously out of step with contemporary values, is overwhelmingly conservative by nature. He observed (1908:18-19):

> The greatest possible difference in conduct between a genius and his contemporaries is so small that it is always difficult to persuade the people who are in daily contact with the gifted one that he is anybody in particular: all the instances to the contrary (Gorki scandalizing New York, for example) being cases in which the genius is in conflict, not with contemporary feeling in his own class, but with some institution which is far behind the times, like the institution of marriage in Russia (to put it no nearer home). In really contemporary situations, your genius is ever 1 part genius and 99 parts Tory.

Because the genius, in his conduct and expression of opinion, is typically in conflict only with some institution that is "far behind the times," observed Shaw (1908:19), "it is necessary for the welfare of society that genius should be privileged to utter sedition, to blaspheme, to outrage good taste, to corrupt the youthful mind, and, generally, to scandalize its uncles."

Contrary to Shaw and other spokesmen for the sanity of genius, who stressed the beneficent function of extraordinary men, were those who assessed the genius as essentially diseased and pathological. These advocates of the pathology position were, overwhelmingly, concerned with the genius' great potential for disruptiveness and focused on his inherent revolutionary and dangerously irresponsible nature. The man of genius, observed Lombroso (1891), "being essentially original and a lover of originality, is the natural enemy of traditions and conservatism: he is the born revolutionary, the precursor and the most active pioneer of revolutions" (Lombroso:335). Normal men must fear this "hater of old things and ardent lover of the new and the unknown" (Lombroso:335), Lombroso cautioned, because the genius' ideas are almost inevitably the expressions of an unbalanced and afflicted mind; and, his ideas, not always easily perceived as dangerous, may receive popular acclaim and become transformed into historical fact (Lombroso:xi). In 1932, Henry T.F. Rhodes, a member of the International Academy of Criminology, shifted from the typical assessment of mental disturbance in the great man and defined the psychology of genius as inherently criminal. The overpowering need to be original—treated by Rhodes as an innate deficiency in men of genius—is responsible for the genius' "sublime hatred" for all existing social arrangements. Unlike the ordinary man who "capitulates" and comes to terms with society, observed Rhodes, the genius either cannot or will not do so; and those who do not conform to the dictates of society are, "when all is said and done, actual or potential criminals" (1932:59). As such, the man of genius is "the greatest enemy of society, and in consequence it is society's method to destroy the genius first and [not infrequently] adopt his criminal theories afterwards" (1932:52). Occasionally, however, cautioned Rhodes, the genius prevails and "destroys society" (1932:52).

What distinguished those assessments of genius that defined the great man as a "blessing" and a responsible agent of progress and modernity from those that viewed him as a fundamentally dangerous and unstable element in the history of man, was the tendency of the latter to regard the genius' alleged propensity for dangerous thought and action as rooted in a pathological condition. The genius, more than most other men, was seen as a victim of compulsion—a compulsion dictated by his own particular constitution. His works were, therefore, the expressions not of well-reasoned intention or choice, but, instead, the products of a mind—bent on originality—which lacked the elements necessary to impose "responsible" direction.

Unlike the Romantics, therefore, who regarded the genius' impulse for novel expression as evidence of a mysterious origin and a peculiar relation to the divine, the "scientific" assessments of pathology defined this need for originality as an indicator of an unstable condition. This need for producing the original, especially when subject to other anomalies of the organism, was believed to give expression to the multitude of those eccentricities and divergences from accepted norms that were said to characterize most men of genius. To Lombroso, for example, it is primarily their impulse for novelty that has fostered among modern men of genius the tendency to express themselves in ways that are indicative of a "morbid" constitution. Not always able to satisfy their need for originality within the context of established rules, geniuses succumb, observed Lombroso, to a large variety of undesirable tendencies; the result is symbolism, mysticism, obscenities, an undue "minuteness of detail" in literature, failure to paint in perspective, and "strange punctuation" in their writing. Commenting specifically on the "total absence of perspective in many modern paintings," Lombroso assessed this failure as a "kind of atavism explicable by arrested development of some one organ" (Lombroso:200). Nordau, quite similarly, explained "the curious style of certain recent painters" —impressionists, "stipplers," "papilloteurs," "dyers in gray and faded tints," and so forth—as the distortions imposed by a pathological condition called "nystagmus," or "trembling of the eyeball" (Nordau:27). "The painters who assure us that they are sincere, and reproduce nature as they see it, speak the truth," observed Nordau, for, in fact, they "perceive the phenomena of nature trembling, restless, [and] devoid of firm outline" (Nordau:27).

This tendency, common in the mad genius literature, to link certain types of artistic and intellectual expression with various forms and degrees of pathology, deserves to be seen as an attempt to control or monitor the direction of intellectual change and innovation. The genius, acknowledged as a uniquely "gifted" being and possessor of a powerful impulse for originality, was the holder of a "license" permitting him to "blaspheme" and challenge established rules and authorities and, in that sense, help "guide" the course of civilization. However, the profusion of styles and schools of thought in every artistic and intellectual endeavor during the nineteenth and twentieth centuries created a profoundly chaotic situation that challenged not only formal rules and arrangements, but saw the advocates of competing styles and ideologies hopelessly in discord.[5] Hence, the obvious questions arose. Who, of the men of genius, are the true "prophets" of the age? And who, perhaps even more importantly, are the false? The artists, philosophers, political theorists—the men of genius themselves—appeared incapable of elucidation and their intended clarifications only amplified existing confusion. Instead, it was primarily the physician-psychiatrist who was willing and appeared capable of resolving this dilemma. Trained in the latest "scientific" methods of discerning the diseased from the normal, and granted the authority to exercise this training in judging the health of others, it was the medical professional who assumed the challenge of evaluating the works of genius.

The attempt to monitor the direction and degree of change during the nineteenth and twentieth centuries, however, was aimed not at all products of "innovations" of men of genius, but remained confined, generally, to those intellectual pursuits with more clearly ethical and cultural implications. N. K. Royse, for example, who saw the genius as pathology prone, argued in terms highly reminiscent of Fontenelle and others who believed the potential for "true" progress to be confined to specific intellectual concerns. While concurring, at least in principle, with the conventional view that the distinguishing mark of genius is his originality, Royse recognized a finite potential for profound originality. He observed (1891:299-300):

> The human mind is finite, and therefore is not susceptible of infinite expansion. In not a few directions, it would appear the utmost limit of human achievement has long ago been reached; and what the race has since been able to accomplish in these directions has fallen, and most probably ever will fall, more or less below the high-tide marks of by-gone days.

Importantly, however, Royse believed two areas of intellectual endeavor to be exempt from the limitation to further "expansion"—the areas of "scientific discovery" and "mechanical invention." In these, observed Royse (1891:305), the "gate of opportunity" remains wide open to "ambitions" and enterprising men of genius. He noted (1891: 310):

The two lines of human pursuit still unimpoverished by use—or, to put it more positively, still widening, growing deeper, and increasing in height and length of opportunities for investigation— are the various sciences, and the utilization of the truths and principles derived therefrom in divers mechanical inventions.

Satisfactory as this situation may prove to the scientists and inventors, observed Royse, "it is wholly discouraging to all other classes of intellectual toilers—that vast multitude of men of letters and of aesthetics" (1891:307). For these others it meant, in fact, that none could ever hope to equal, much less surpass, the most accomplished works of former greats. As Royce noted, "the geniuses who may yet arise in these branches must be inferior to those who have already flourished" (1891:310).[6]

The attempt to relegate the accomplishments in contemporary art, literature, and philosophic speculation to secondary status was rooted in the assumption of certain fixed regulations of style and decorum in all fields of intellectual endeavor. To W. Hirsch, for example, the works of Realists and Naturalists are of a clearly inferior quality due to the failure of their creators to perceive "that the task of art and literature is to ennoble the taste of the public" (1897:216). On the contrary, he observed, these individuals "speculate on the baser impulses and evil qualities of the rabble" and amuse themselves with what is "dirty" and "vulgar" (1897:216-217). And Nordau (1900), a foremost critic of modern artistic expression, exclaimed:

> New forms! Are not the ancient forms flexible and ductile enough to lend expression to every sentiment and every thought? Has a true poet ever found any difficulty in pouring into known and standard forms that which surged within him, and demanded an issue? [Nordau:544]

The "ancient forms," then, to Nordau, were judged "flexible" and "ductile" enough to accommodate every "true" man of genius. In reality, however, the "legitimate" degree of flexibility proved relatively narrow, as demonstrated by Nordau's appraisal of Holman Hunt's "Shadow of the Cross." Nordau observed:

> In this picture Christ is standing in the Oriental attitude of prayer with outstretched arms, and the shadow of his body, falling on the ground, shows the form of a cross. Here we have a most instructive pattern of the processes of mystic thought. Holman

Hunt imagines Christ in prayer. Through the association of ideas there awakes in him simultaneously the mental image of Christ's subsequent death on the cross. He wants, by the instrumentality of painting, to make the association of these ideas visible. And hence he lets the living Christ throw a shadow which assumes the form of a cross, thus foretelling the fate of the Saviour, as if some mysterious, incomprehensible power had so posed his body with respect to the rays of the sun that a wondrous annunciation of his destiny must needs write itself on the floor. [Nordau:86]

This style of presentation, continued Nordau, is not the "sober vision" of an "Old Master," for it seeks to arouse emotions through "mysterious allusions" and "obscure symbols" that have "nothing to do with the reproduction of visible reality" (Nordau:85). Instead,

If an Old Master had had to paint the same idea, namely, the praying Christ filled with the presentiment of his impending death, he would have shown us in the picture a realistic Christ in prayer, and in a corner an equally realistic crucifixion; but he would never have sought to blend both these different scenes into a single one by a shadowy connection. [Nordau:86]

"This," concluded Nordau, "is the difference between the religious painting of the strong healthy believer and of the emotional degenerate mind" (Nordau:86).

The endeavors to control or guide the intellectual climate during the late nineteenth and early twentieth centuries were not confined, however, to artistic and literary expression; they were likewise directed to developments in political thought and social criticism. Comparable to the attention focused on artists and authors who "failed" to adhere to established forms and rules of decorum, the sense of "alarm" was reserved for those men of genius—identified commonly as "revolutionists," "anarchists," and "leaders of subversive movements"—who displayed a "flagrant" disregard for established authorities and existing political and social arrangements.[7] And frequently, in fact, the alleged interferences with existing conditions were described as constituting violations of fixed and legitimate "laws" or "principles" pertaining to moral, political, or economic life.[8] Identical to the explanations provided about the artistic or literary genius who infringed upon established rules, the genius who displayed his "antisocial habit of mind" in the areas of political and social speculation was defined as a victim of organic or psychological impairment. The expressions of "dangerous" or "revolutionary" ideas were regarded not as volitional acts of innovation or defiance, but were believed to be dictated by a "morbid" constitution. And Nordau concurred with Lombroso:

> It can scarcely be doubted that the writings and acts of revolutionists and anarchists are also attributable to degeneracy. The degenerate is incapable of adapting himself to existing circumstances. This incapacity, indeed, is an indication of morbid variation in every species, and probably a primary cause of their sudden extinction. He therefore rebels against conditions and views of things which he necessarily feels to be painful, chiefly because they impose upon him the duty of self-control, of which he is incapable on account of his organic weakness of will. Thus he becomes an improver of the world. [Nordau:22]

The dominant view, then, during the course of the madness-genius controversy, conceived of the great man, and particularly the contemporary nonscientific genius, as an often reckless and dangerous "improver" of the world.[9] Consistent with the highly deterministic tendencies in the behavioral sciences during the nineteenth and early part of the twentieth centuries, the genius' apparent lack of appreciation for the sanctity of established rules and regulations was defined as rooted in an inherently unstable physico-psychological constitution. And, once defined as an essentially unbalanced and pathological subject disposed to irresponsible thought and action, it was but a logical extension to propose that the "uninformed" public deserves "protection" from the most "dangerous" of the contemporary "greats."

Most frequently, this expressed concern for the general public took the form of "alerting" the reader to those men whose intellectual products were evaluated as the expressions of "unstable" and "sick" minds. In a few instances, however, specific proposals were designed to "neutralize" the most dangerous among the "irresponsibles." Nordau argued, for example, that the police, the public prosecutor, and the criminal judge are not the proper "protectors of society" against the "crimes committed with pen and paper," due to the tendency of these men to "infuse into their mode of proceeding too much consideration for interests not always . . . those of cultivated and moral man" (Nordau:557-558). Instead, he recommended, it is the "medical specialists of insanity" who must move into the forefront in the struggle against the "enemies of society" (Nordau:559). To do this, they must join existing organizations such as the "Association of Men for the Suppression of Immorality" and the "Society for Ethical Culture." Through this and other means, they must enlighten all "cultivated persons" and demonstrate to them the "mental derangement" of many contemporary artists and authors (Nordau:558). It is the medically trained specialist, observed Nordau, who is best equipped to implement a program of "prophylactics" that must include such measures as the "characterization of the leading degenerates as mentally diseased," the "unmasking and stigmatizing of their imitators as enemies of society," and warning the public "against the lies of these parasites" (Nordau:560). The enemy must be defeated. Through these methods, Nordau reasoned, both the "work and man would be annihilated" and "no respectable bookseller would keep the condemned book; no respectable paper would mention it, or give the author access to its columns; no respectable family would permit the branded work to be in their house" (Nordau:559).

Nordau's ideas were not, however, particularly extreme. A program was issued by Theo. B. Hyslop in 1925 that involved a "complete revision of our methods of certification, classification, and administration" of the mentally ill. Specifically, it recommended the classification of the mentally sick as either "Responsibles" or "Irresponsibles" and urged the forced confinement of only the "Irresponsibles"—or those who in their thought or behavior "have become subversive and a source of danger to the individual or to the community" (1925: 276-281). Predictably, the men of genius, identified as the "great abnormals," figured prominently in Hyslop's list of "irresponsibles."[10]

The evolvement of the modern conception of genius during the eighteenth century, then, with its pronounced stress on "originality," with the accompanying disdain for "mere" imitation and the contentment with established forms and ideas, deserves to be seen as a culminating point in the century's long debate regarding the ability of modern man to surpass the most profound achievements of the ancients. Initially the "discovery" of the advocates of modernity and progress, the notion of the "Originalgenie" received popular acclaim during the Romantic era. It is the enthusiastic endorsement of the idea of genius at the turn of the eighteenth century that established "originality" as the foremost criterion for all intellectual and artistic production. However, the post-Napoleonic period, informed by the "excesses" of the French Revolution and experiencing the revolutionary activity of 1820, 1830, and 1848-1849, saw the emergence of an increasingly reactionary mood and a growing tendency to view the "Originalgenie" as a potentially dangerous and unstabilizing force. Unlike the Romantics, who regarded the genius as an embodiment of some supernatural force, the more established interests during the Metternich era were far less inclined to view the genius as a "law unto himself." Especially when acting in the role of commentator of contemporary culture and interpreter of contemporary experience, the genius became increasingly perceived as a dangerously irresponsible agent who issued broad and uncompromising judgments. Indeed, to many observers the "lessons" of recent history appeared to be quite clear—the genius' frequent fondness for broad generalizations and abstract theories, combined with his contempt for practical considerations, revealed him as a dominant force in the causation of "disasterous" and "catastrophic" social and political revolutions.

Tocqueville, for example, commenting specifically on the role of the French men of letters in "fermenting" the Revolution of 1789, made the following observations in *The Old Regime and the French Revolution:*

> Their very way of living [the men of letters] led these writers to indulge in abstract theories and generalizations regarding the nature of government, and to place a blind confidence in these. For living as they did, quite out of touch with practical politics, they lacked the experience which might have tempered their enthusiasms. Thus they completely failed to perceive the very real obstacles in the way of even the most salutary revolutions. [in Huszar, 1960:13]

> Our revolutionaries [the men of letters] had the same fondness for broad generalizations, cut-and-dried legislative systems, and a pedantic symmetry; the same contempt for hard facts; the same taste for reshaping institutions on novel, ingenious, original lines. ... The result was nothing short of disasterous; for what is a merit in the writer may well be a vice in the statesman and the very qualities which go to make great literature can lead to catastrophic revolutions. [in Huszar:18]

The start of the mad genius controversy toward the middle of the nineteenth century, then, appears tied to the revolutionary unrest of the period and, more specifically, to the recognition that those identified as geniuses often tended to occupy a central position in fermenting social, political, and intellectual unrest. The evaluation of the men of genius in terms of sanity and madness constituted one response to the perceived influence of many of these individuals; it served to alert the public not only to all geniuses in general, but identified, in particular, those in whom the degree of pathology was judged to be most advanced.[11] That such evaluation of the genius should have been conducted in this context of pathology was primarily a consequence of existing notions concerning the nature of the extraordinary man. Given the commonality of the belief that sanity and health are found not in the disproportionate exercise of a single faculty, but, instead, in the harmonious interplay of certain specific mental powers, the Romantics' redefinition of the great man, as one who derives his vitality from a heavily dominant imagination, did much to establish a logical foundation for the association of genius and madness. In addition, the supposed involuntariness and semiconsciousness of intellectual production supported the existing idea that foremost intellectual accomplishments are the products of minds somehow eccentric, unbalanced, compulsive, and possibly diseased. Finally, the genius, far from trying to disassociate himself from the accepted elements of madness, often spoke in confusing terms about his melancholic temperament, his "mania," and his "divine inspiration"; further, he not infrequently confessed to his own ill health. All that appeared necessary to "substantiate" as scientific fact the long suspected marginality of the genius' mental condition was the presentation of pertinent empirical data. The description and evaluation of given artistic and intellectual products were believed to provide such empirical support.

Given the long-standing speculation concerning the sanity of the artistic and intellectually prominent individual, and adding certain prevailing notions pertaining to the nature of the extraordinary man, the "problem" of the genius suggested itself as a legitimate medical concern. That the "scientific" verdicts of sanity and ill health were to a considerable degree the expression of the labelers' endorsement or disapproval of given intellectual products of men of genius is consistent with the currently accepted position that social control considerations constitute an integral part in the labeling of madness, and, indeed, have figured prominently in the very development of the mental health movement.

The contention that the modern mental health movement was initiated and to a degree has been maintained for purposes of social control, while shared by such observers as Phyllis Chesler (1972), R. D. Laing (1964, 1969, 1972), and Aaron Esterson (1964), finds its clearest and most historical explication in Thomas Szasz (particularly 1961 and 1970).[1][2] While the concept of mental illness is ancient, only during the seventeenth century, argues Szasz, did European society organize a movement based on it. The movement—the ostensible aim of which was to protect society and its members from harm—was "Institutional Psychiatry" (Szasz, 1970:4). The fact that this movement followed on the heels of the Inquisition is, to Szasz, no mere coincidence. It simply demonstrates the transformation of a religious ideology into a scientific one, where the "persecution" of mental patients replaced the former persecution of heretics (1970:xx). Whereas prior to the eighteenth century, refusal or failure to affirm society's dominant values led to such labelings as witch and heretic, thereafter such nonconformity gradually became redefined as a public health matter necessitating stigmatization, treatment, involuntary confinement or hospitalization, and the suspension of an individual's rights and privileges (1970:13).[1][3] When viewed in the light of social control, observes Szasz, the definition of psychiatry as a medical specialty concerned with the study, diagnosis, and treatment of mental illness is misleading. The psychiatrist is not concerned exclusively with mental illnesses per se, but, quite importantly, serves as an "interpreter of moral rules and enforcer of social laws and expectations" (Szasz, 1967:16). What betrays the psychiatrist's function as an agent of social control, argues Szasz, is his tendency to sacrifice his loyalty to the individual patient in order to provide support for such powerful institutions as government, schools, and industry (Szasz, 1967:23).[1][4] Indeed, he argues, the field of "institutional psychiatry is . . . designed to protect and uplift the groups (the family, the State), by persecuting and degrading the individual (as insane or ill)" (Szasz, 1970:xxv).

No doubt, without the expansion and legitimation of the mental health movement during the nineteenth and twentieth centuries, the typing of the multitude of geniuses as mentally disturbed might have been considerably more difficult if, perhaps, not impossible. The participation in the genius dialogue of a large number of individuals from the medical-psychiatric profession served to provide a societal aura to the polemic and helped establish the verdict of pathology as scientific fact. The charge that many, if not all, men of genius were victims of pathology served to discredit them and their intellectual and artistic products and, quite importantly, placed the generally acknowledged moral authority of the genius into serious question. The majority consensus of pathology during the period of the genius controversy proved to be an effective antidote to the often ecstatic celebration of the great man and the supporters of the Romantic spirit of that time. However, the assertion presented earlier—that the linking with pathology of especially those men of genius who were most "flagrant" in their transgressions of certain artistic or intellectual conventions constituted an attempt to discredit these individuals and, in this way, served to control the dynamic of change—while essentially correct, must now be refined.

While those who sought to establish the "scientific" connection between genius and madness often revealed themselves, in the words of Szasz, as the "interpreters(s) of moral rules and enforcer(s) of social laws and expectations," the conclusion that the negative typing of the genius had its primary origin in the desire to discredit his frequently "unacceptable" intellectual product is, perhaps, too one-sided. The labelers, as more or less typical products of their age, employed in their analyses, as has been stressed throughout this study, the then current intellectual concepts, categories, and general cultural axioms. Accordingly, they proceeded not only from an existing constellation of essentially Romantic premises pertaining to the nature of the genius, the dynamics of original productivity, and general intellectual processes, and, in this sense, "inherited" a theoretical foundation for the pathlogical condition of the genius; but, additionally, they operated from widely accepted "scientific" assumptions particular to the nineteenth and the early part of the twentieth centuries. The unmistakable tendency, therefore, to interpret all kinds of "strange," "unusual," or "deviant" artistic and intellectual expressions as symptomatic of illness did, indeed, serve the function of social control. But it is important to note that this tendency also developed as a natural outgrowth of a predominantly deterministic framework of human behavior, and the general belief in a statistically normal or average man as the foremost exemplar of sanity and health.

The Romantic men of genius, in their attempt to disassociate themselves from the intellectual and artistic control of their predecessors, ironically made almost inevitable the direct control of themselves and their heirs by their contemporaries. Those trained in "modern" methods of evaluating sanity found, in the self-identifying ideas of the geniuses themselves, the fertile grounds out of which grew their own insights.

NOTES

1. For an authoritative discussion of the debates on the imitation of Cicero and Plato see Zilsel, 1926:214-231.

2. George R. Havens makes the interesting observation that Fontenelle's qualified support of the moderns was one of the reasons for the opposition that for a long time prevented his nomination to the French Academy (1966:84).

3. As Zilsel observes, the genius ideal, in its very conception, constitutes the embodiment of natural and instinctive originality, and an uncompromising "Autoritätsfeindlichkeit," or an inherent need to oppose tradition and authority (1918:144).

4. Zilsel (1918) proposes the interesting thesis that the nineteenth and twentieth centuries' veneration of great men had the function of fostering not originality in intellectual production, but promoted, instead, an imitation of the most highly acclaimed men of genius. Zilsel perceives this development as ironic, because it stands in sharp contradiction to the very essence of genius—the relentless pursuit of the novel.

5. In the area of painting alone, for example, the late nineteenth and early twentieth centuries produced a wide variety of styles or fashions and included such developments as impressionism, intimism, fauvism, cubism, futurism, expressionism, dadaism, surrealism, orphism, vorticism, and purism.

As Ian Dunlap stresses in *The Shock of the New* (1972), the common initial reaction to most of these new expressions in art was to discredit them as evidence of madness.

6. Turning to the state of contemporary poetry, for instance, Royse concluded that the last half century has failed to produce a single noteworthy contribution. He observed (1891:303):

For poetry simple, sensuous, sonorous; for poetry that takes possession of the whole being—the eye by its form, the ear by its music, the mind by its symbolism—for this supremest of human products, one must have recourse to days gone by.

7. A striking exception to this rule, in this study's sample, is Schwarz (1916), who, as an exception to the general pattern applied the labels of ill-health and madness to geniuses who displayed a "blind reverence for official or institutional wisdom, for conventions, traditions, (and) precedents" (Schwarz:386). By comparison, the "vigorous," "healthy," and "sane" man of genius was defined by Schwarz as one whose mind was "turned to the future" and promoted "realism . . . economic determinism, worship of humanity, democracy, popularization of knowledge, socialism, communism, anarchism, cooperation, fairness, sincerity, (and) reverence for logic or reason" (Schwarz:386-387). The label of pathology, therefore, while it was applied in the overwhelming number of cases to certain "undesirable" novel developments, was similarly used to discredit those minds who "turned to the past" and conformed to more traditional rules and ideas.

8. Typical of this tendency is Nordau's charge that Tolstoy's "morbid fraternal love," his "irrational philanthropy," and advocacy of an "impotent socialism" stand in contradiction to "all economic and moral laws" (Nordau:170).

9. The scientifically oriented intellectual or man of genius was not perceived as particularly dangerous in the writings of the genius-madness controversy. Overwhelmingly, the concern was with the genius who enjoyed a relatively high degree of freedom from institutional restraints and, as a commentator on contemporary culture and interpreter of contemporary experience, often made sweeping and uncompromising judgments about societal values. Clearly, however, as Bennett Berger (1957) points out in his discussion of societal stereotypes regarding the sociologist, there is an established tradition in Western society that views the scientifically inclined intellectual with considerable apprehension. The idea of the mad scientist and such creations as Frankenstein's monster are, in Berger's judgment, the warnings of the literary intellectual who regards the attempt to study man and society in "objective" or "value-free terms" as leading toward a type of depersonalized world foreshadowed in *1984* and *Brave New World*.

10. We are told, for example, that the "subversivist" Lenin and other Bolsheviks contributed to the "poisoning" of the minds of the Russian people. Hyslop observed: "Lenin was undoubtedly affected mentally, and he has but served as a text for the Russian 'Toms O'Bedlam' who now act as his imitators. Viewed in the light of history, other despots have perverted the moral instincts of the Russian people, and there has been a throw-back to barbarism owing to the initiative of a disordered mind" (1925: xiv).

11. Other means of "controlling" prominent intellectuals existed, of course. One such means consisted of recruiting intellectuals to controllable positions of prominence in the government hierarchy and in state supported institutions of research and higher learning. Fritz Ringer's insightful analysis of the German "mandarin" intellectuals (1969)—identified as a group of university professors and government officials—clearly suggests the existence of boundaries beyond which a "mandarin" intellectual could not step.

12. Unlike traditional psychiatric theory that adheres to a medical or individual system model of mental illness, Chesler, Szasz, Laing, and Esterson regard mental illness as a response to difficulties encountered in interpersonal, family relations, and other involvements in power situations. Illustrating this, Laing and Esterson (1964) see most schizophrenic symptoms as constituting rebellious behavior directed at tyrannical and unreasonable parents. Accordingly, the families of patients are more aptly termed "sick," while the patients' symptoms constitute more or less "normal" reactions to highly unusual circumstances. In a similar line of argument, Chesler (1972) takes the position that schizophrenia in families is best understood in terms of sex-role alienation or sex-role rejection. In cases of partial or total rejection of her socially devalued female role, argues Chesler, the "rebellious" female challenges the privileged status and power of her male parent or husband and invites the label of "madness" that serves as a means of social control.

13. The fact that the French "hôspital général," the German "Irrenhaus," and the English "madhouse" performed important social control functions from the time of their founding serves to support Szasz's contention. The confinement of the mentally ill, along with vagabonds, criminals, and other "undesirables," asserts Foucault (1973:49), constituted one of the answers the seventeenth cen-

tury provided to an economic crisis in the Western World that was characterized by the reduction of wages, unemployment, and scarcity of coinage. It is in this way that those designated mad became subject to the same rules of forced labor as the destitute and the criminal (1973: 58). The royal decree that provided for the founding of the "Hôspital Général" of Paris in 1656 clearly underscores the social control functions intended. The economic objectives were to increase manufactures, provide work for the able-bodied, and reduce unemployment. The social functions were concerned with the punishment of willful idleness, the restorations of public order, and the elimination of begging. And finally, the moral purposes were to relieve the needy, the ill, and the suffering, and to deal with immorality and antisocial behavior (Rosen, 1969:162-163). The fact that the "Hôspital Général" housed sick people, old people, epileptics, and the mentally ill meant, observes Rosen, that "in the course of time the general hospital combined the characteristics of a penal institution, an asylum, a workshop, and a hospital" (1969:163).

14. For an explication of this charge see Szasz's discussion of the college psychiatrist as a "double agent" and instrument of control (October 1967).

Conclusion

A Discussion of the Labeling Paradigm

This study has taken a historical phenomenon as its organizing concern—the mad genius controversy of the nineteenth and twentieth centuries—and defined it as a problem in the sociology of deviance. Presented with a change in the prevailing conception of genius from "sane" during the eighteenth century to "mad" during the nineteenth, the polemic of genius and madness suggested itself as an ideal subject for the exploration of certain aspects pertaining to the dynamics of negative typing as they apply, not only to select individuals, but to an entire category of persons—those identified as men of genius. Importantly, the decision to adopt an "agnostic" stance with regard to the question of the genius' madness—a position consistent with the labeling perspective in sociology—has enabled the investigator to focus on the beliefs and attitudes pertaining to mental illness without necessarily having to endorse or reject these himself. Freed from the more traditional clinical preoccupation with the individual "patient," the investigator has been permitted to pursue the larger social concerns relating to mental illness and, in this way, explore the "causes" or determinants of negative typing. On the most general level, this study has sought to ascertain the pivotal developments and changes in Western culture responsible for the transformation of the once-prevailing conception of genius. The findings of this study warrant some critical observations about the process of negative typing in general and, more specifically, about the labeling paradigm current in sociology.

Central to the labeling perspective in the sociology of deviance and social control is the pronounced theoretical concern with social "process." As such, deviance is viewed not as a static phenomenon consisting of discrete acts of "wrongdoing" or departures from normative expectations, but as subject to patterns and processes of social interaction between deviants and nondeviants that involve conflicting values, a language of labels, and social reactions. The conception of deviance as an ongoing, continuously shifting product of dynamic social processes between rule-violators and others has led to a shift in emphasis from the individual "flaws" or attributes of the deviant to a concern with the societal reaction to those attributes. Accordingly, the questions raised are how, why, and with what consequences certain individuals or groups define given behaviors as deviant, abnormal, or criminal. Unlike the more "clinical" examinations of deviance that concentrate on the characteristics of the rule-violator, the labeling orientation focuses instead on the characteristics of the "controllers"—the rule-makers, the labelers, and the agencies of social control. This shift in emphasis is reflected in the labeling-oriented literature in its focus on how deviance is "created" through acts of rule-making, and on demonstrating the selective nature of rule-enforcement and the application of deviant labels.[1] But while this expressed concern for the social reaction to rule-breaking may be justified operationally, the reduced emphasis on the rule-violator can lead to serious distortions and omissions in our understanding of deviance and the dynamics of typing (see Gibbs, 1966; and Lorber, 1967).

It is perhaps an oversimplification to suggest that the labeling approach ignores questions specific to the deviant; certainly, its premise that deviants and those who label and process them are always engaged in a complimentary relationship precludes such omission on theoretical grounds. However, in labeling studies where the deviant is submitted to examination, such focus is generally in terms only of victimization, adjustments to typing, and identity management. The concern is with the sequence of interaction following the initial acts of rule-breaking and labeling, and the gradual changes in the behavior and self-concept experienced by the labeled to correspond with the deviant status assigned by others.[2] What receives little or no attention in the labeling literature is a view of the rule-violator preceding the act of labeling and processing by agents of social control. Hence, omitted are data pertaining to the activities, motivations, and self-view of the individual rule-breakers prior to formal or informal acts of stigmatization (Lorber, 1967: 302).

It is this omission in the labeling literature that results in a distorted view of the processes involved in labeling and the acquisition of deviant identities. It fosters a view of the "typical" deviant as a more or less passive individual who, after an initially perceived departure from some normative expectation, is "victimized" by negative typing, stigmatization, and punishment; the deviant is portrayed as one who submits or reacts to externally imposed pressures and, in the process, undergoes key changes in his self-concept. Given the bias of most labeling studies—one that stresses the societal reaction to rule-breaking—certain findings are virtually precluded. They include the following: (1) negative typing may be initiated and promoted by the "victim"; and (2) a deviant identity may in fact precede labeling by others. This study views these as important considerations.

As the examination of the monographs on the genius controversy has revealed, the modern association of genius with madness was rooted, to a considerable degree, in the pronouncements issued in support of this association by numerous men of genius. Far from having been the passive victims or responders to negative typing, a sizable proportion of, in particular, Romantic geniuses acted as the initiators of their "victimization," and more or less deliberately conveyed an impression that contributed to the "imposition" by others of the "madness" label. These Romantic men of genius underscored by their actions and the numerous instances of self-labeling that the ancient commentators had indeed been correct in their observation that the "demon of madness" was no stranger to the extraordinarily gifted individual. These "confessions" and the largely willful projection of the image of madness were motivated, so it has been argued, by at least two dominant and interrelated factors: the need for an affirmed identity, and the need to break from the dependence on the past.

Generally impoverished and deprived of political power and a privileged class status following the demise of the ancien régime, the Romantic artists and men of letters revived the classical notion of "divine mania" or "inspiration" and established it as a defining mark of the extraordinary individual. The aura of "mania" endowed the genius with a mystical and inexplicable quality that served to differentiate him from the typical man, the bourgeois, the philistine, and, quite importantly, the "mere" man of talent; it established him as the modern heir of the ancient Greek poet and seer and, like his classical counterpart, enabled him to claim some of the powers and privileges granted to the "divinely possessed" and "inspired." To the Romantics, the idea of "mania" conveyed the notions of "possession," suffering, and "Weltschmerz," and the display of these qualities served to affirm his identity.

The appropriation of certain supposed qualities of the ancients had to be effected, however, without assuming a subservient role to traditional authority. This necessitated a redefinition of genius. To create a new independence, genius no longer could be seen in the Enlightenment terms of balance, proportion, and a synthesis of mental powers, but exclusively in terms of originality—a quality that demanded an unfettering of the imagination from the constraints of judgment, sense, taste, and memory. The idea met both criteria: it not only, through its stress on the irrational imagination, made possible the appropriation of "mania" from the past, but it did so while insuring independence in the present. There was, however, a critical by-product: while the new definition liberated them from the past, it also disassociated them from the very qualities that traditionally had been seen as establishing and safeguarding sanity—and the irony is that they could not disassociate themselves from this perspective. They came to see their own madness as inevitable.

The need, then, to seek a sense of identity by appropriating certain qualities of the ancients and the need, simultaneously, to establish their own intellectual and artistic independence led them to adopt a system of premises and logic that left them defenseless against the label of madness. Trapped by their own logic, they had no recourse—they assumed the label themselves.

The findings derived from this study of the genius-madness controversy, then, demonstrate the fact that the individual may possess a "deviant" identity prior to formal or informal acts of stigmatization by others and, more or less deliberately, may seek to convey an impression of himself that he hopes will lead to the imposition of a particular label by his audience. The identity that had been sought by especially the Romantics was in terms of the sacred and inspired "mania" of the ancients. While these Romantics seemed successful in establishing this particular image of the genius during their age, their expressed doubts and trepidation helped foster, in subsequent years, a nonmystical and "scientific" assessment that stressed not "mania," but clinical pathology as the condition of genius. What is significant about the genius-madness controversy, however, for purposes of this discussion, is not that the attempt to negotiate a particular identity had "backfired," but that the genius was clearly not the helpless "victim" of philistine labelers—he not only contributed heavily to his "victimization," he even, to a degree, instigated it.

The extent, of course, to which all forms of deviant behavior evolve from processes of self-typing and the manipulation of a public image by the "deviants" themselves remains an empirical question. Given the currently accepted position, however, that deviance and the typing as such are the result of "negotiation" (that is, a reciprocal interaction process in which deviant and other take turns acting and reacting),[3] the common portrayal of the deviant in the labeling literature—as a more or less helpless "victim" who submits or, at best, reacts to sanctions imposed by powerful others—is, by necessity, a distortion that has consequences for an understanding of deviance. Importantly, the "compassionate" or "underdog" view of deviance, which focuses on the "creation" of deviance through the selective application of labels by superordinate others, obscures a recognition of several factors that may be significant in the study of most deviant activity: (1) the deviant is generally an initiator of labeling processes through willful rule-breaking; (2) the rule-breaking may instigate or, perhaps, reflect a legitimatizing view of self;[4] and (3) this view may cause him to manipulate, encourage, and even assist in the labeling by others.[5]

The sociological framework best designed to explore the relation of an actor's identity and self-typing to subsequent public labeling is, so it seems, the labeling paradigm. In accordance with the basic theoretical vocabulary of the labeling perspective—derived from symbolic interactionism—self-identification is conceived as intimately related to social or public identification, and the actor's self-view is defined as instrumental in shaping his lines of action (see Schur, 1971:8, 19). As such, the labeling paradigm acknowledges, theoretically, the importance of understanding the activities, motivations, and self-view of the rule-breaker preceding rule-breaking and the subsequent act of labeling by others.

While the labeling paradigm theoretically recognizes the necessity of examining the "contributions" of both rule-breaker and others in the causation of deviance, labeling oriented studies have focused, overwhelmingly, on how deviance is "created" by rule-makers, labelers, and agencies of social control, and portray the deviant as a victim of reaction processes (Nettler, 1974:202-212). Howard Becker (1967) for example, a foremost exponent of the labeling model, has justified this tendency in labeling studies on grounds that the deviant is frequently "more sinned against than sinning" (Becker:101) and that, traditionally, "a great many more studies are biased in the direction of the interests of responsible officials than the other way around" (Becker: 104).

The political and moral considerations, however, which apparently have been dictating a need to balance the ostensible one-sidedness of the more traditional examinations of deviance by equally one-sided labeling studies favorable to the deviant, make unlikely a balanced exploration of how the actor's motives and self-view contribute to his "victimization." Given the importance of self-initiated typing in the area of deviance[6] and the fact that the labeling paradigm is best designed to study the dynamics of self-typing, the political preference to engage in labeling studies that present an "underdog" view of deviance[7] could prove deterimental and leave this concern unattended or under-explored. The intellectual obligation of sociologist—to understand fully—should dictate a reappraisal of the political disposition to provide interpretations of deviance confined to a perspective of the deviant's victimization by powerful others.[8]

The politically motivated preference in labeling studies for focusing on the "controllers" in the "creation" of deviance has the potential for yet another distortion. Proceeding from an assumption of the labeling perspective that rule-making and the enforcement of rules are selective processes that reflect, quite frequently, self-serving purposes, labeling studies have placed a dominant emphasis on the behavior and motives of rule-makers and rule-enforcers. By submitting conventional members of society to examination from a standpoint outside of its respectable confines, a kind of condemnation of these people, if only by implication, has become inevitable. Those "respectable" individuals, seen by sociologists as the labeling others, became, in this perspective, rather negatively labeled themselves.[9]

The inclination to concentrate on the self-serving functions of rule-making and rule-enforcement, while it contributes to the understanding of deviance and labeling in one respect, serves to detract from the importance of other factors specific to the etiology of typing; by doing so, it makes unlikely a systematic and balanced examination of cultural rules in typing and the way the sociocultural environment contributes to the typing of some individuals or groups and not others. With regard to the mad genius polemic, for example, this limitation in scope can lead to the likelihood of placing undue emphasis on the notion of social control, i.e., where labeling is viewed primarily as a means of discrediting men of genius. Indeed, while the issue of control has figured prominently in the course of the genius-madness controversy and, in that sense, confirms the social control assumption of the labeling paradigm, the content analysis of the given monographs has revealed, quite importantly, that certain changes in the sociocultural realm made the association of genius and madness a near necessity. The findings suggest that, in addition to certain sociohistorical developments, changes in a number of fundamental cultural axioms helped foster the association. Specifically, changes in the conception of man, mind, and mental processes, as well as the developing conceptions of collective psychopathology and a statistically average man, virtually precluded the definition of genius as sane during the nineteenth century. Just as the Enlightenment image of the rational and sane genius was derived from certain widely accepted cultural premises, the majority verdict of madness during the nineteenth century had its roots in a new set of equally compelling intellectual and cultural axioms. The eventual drop in the popularity of the genius-madness association, encountered towards the end of the controversy, deserves to be seen consistently as the consequence of a gradual decline of existing premises and the substitution of new ones. Those who, throughout the course of the genius controversy, arrived at the judgment of sanity were seen to have proceeded from an entirely different set of premises and, almost inevitably, arrived at a different conclusion.

In summary, while the labeling perspective has been found to be well suited for the study of the dynamics of negative typing, political considerations—in response to studies that tended to legitimize the labbelers—seem to have created an equally one-sided view in favor of the labeled. This is, however, in violation of an important theoretical premise of the labeling perspective—namely, that patterns and processes of social interaction between labelers and the labeled are central to a study of the dynamics of typing. The labeling perspective does, theoretically, provide what is possibly the best means to address certain problems in typing. To date, however, the application of this perspective has not been without its problems.

This study, while critical of the common employment of the labeling paradigm, nevertheless has adopted certain of its premises in its study of the madness-genius controversy. It has, almost inadvertantly, had the advantage of a historical perspective as well—a perspective that provides sensitivity to shifting intellectual attitudes—through the study of monographs written over a considerable period of time. The result has provided an examination of the subject under study that has incorporated some of the advantages of both perspectives and has attempted, hopefully, to avoid certain shortcomings in the usual employment of either.

NOTES

1. According to this view, all "true" deviance is the consequence of successful typing. "Social groups create deviance," argues Howard Becker, an exponent of the labeling paradigm, "by making the rules whose infraction constitutes deviance, and by applying those rules to particular people and labeling them as outsiders. From this point of view, deviance is not a quality of the act the person commits, but rather a consequence of the application by others of rules and sanctions to an 'offender.' The deviant is one to whom that label has successfully been applied; deviant behavior is behavior that people so label" (1967:3).

The recognition that agencies of social control, due to pressures internal and external to their work situation, are highly selective in their rule enforcement, has led to the assumption that deviance is, in large measure, a consequence of the extent and form of social control. Thus conceived, social control becomes an independent variable or "cause" of deviance rather than the mere effect of the magnitude and variable forms of deviation. Accordingly, as an example, differences in crime rates among communities can be related to variations in available means of policing, as measured by a police to population ratio (see Lemert, 1967:18).

2. Accordingly, the actor's response, linked to the societal reaction to his "deviance" (revolving around stigmatization, punishment, segregation, social control, reward, withdrawal, and so forth, becomes the subject of scrutiny (see Lemert, 1951; 1967). Consistent with this line of inquiry, some of the questions raised are the following: What consequences does the application of a label have for the person typed? How does he come to adopt the deviant role that may be assigned to him? Are there changes in his group memberships? To what extent does he realign his self-conception to accord with the deviant role assigned him? (Rubington and Weinberg, 1971:3-4).

The pronounced emphasis in labeling studies with the deviant in terms of victimization and identity management is reflected in Lemert's distinction between "primary" and "secondary" deviation, a distinction that has been central to the work of recent labeling analysts. While "primary" deviation refers to the sheer act of rule-violation, the term "secondary" deviation is reserved for the individual whose self-conception and activities have come to conform to the deviant image that others have assigned him (see Lemert, 1951:75-78).

3. An illustration of the process of negotiation leading to the label of deviant is provided by Thomas Scheff's "Negotiating Reality" (in *Social Problems,* Summer 1968:3-17).

4. Donald Cressey (1953) found in his study of 333 embezzlers, for example, that, in addition to factors of "need" and "opportunity" to commit the crime, the offense was never committed until the embezzler had developed a rationalization that legitimated the offense to him. As Daniel Glaser (in Rubington and Weinberg, 1971:329) observed: "When frustrated humans perceive a deviant solution to their problems, they seem unable to grasp the solution until they can represent it to themselves in such a manner as to permit them to maintain a favorable conception of themselves. . . . In Cressey's cases, a shift of perspective, often by taking the standpoint of new reference groups, was needed to change the trustworthy person into an embezzler."

See also G. M. Sykes and D. Matza (1957) who suggest that delinquents must develop a variety of rationalizations that "neutralize" their conventional ties and moral scruples before they can commit delinquent acts.

5. The actor's concern with the presentation of self has implications for not only the study of "conventional" roles, argues Orrin E. Klapp (1962), but for deviant behavior as well. Klapp observes: "All kinds of deviant behavior . . . are processes of self-typing—the deviant is not just being antisocial, aggressive, etc. We may well adopt the premise that everyone in modern society is vitally interested in creating a type for himself, the deviant no less than the Philistine (Klapp:3).

6. For a study underscoring the importance of self-initiated typing see C. J. Williams and M. S. Weinberg, *Homosexuals and the Military: A Study of Less than Honorable Discharge* (New York: Harper & Row, 1971).

7. For a statement advocating a one-sided approach to deviance favorable to the deviant see Howard Becker's "Whose Side Are We On?" (*Social Problems,* 1967:239-247), a Presidential address delivered at the annual meeting of the Society for the Study of Social Problems in 1966.

8. It is interesting to note that Howard Becker's forceful advocacy of a politically slanted or "underdog" sociology of deviance has more recently been modified. In "Labelling Theory Reconsidered" (1973:177-211), he proposes that the politically charged designation of "labelling theory" be henceforth discontinued in favor of the "interactionist theory of deviance" (1973:181). Becker argues that by following the injunction of symbolic interactionism—to study all the parties involved in any episode of alleged deviance—the social scientist is automatically led to explore how labelers and agents of social control contribute to the manufacture of deviance (1973:199).

9. Howard Becker clearly acknowledges this to be a consequence of such politically oriented labeling studies (see *Social Problems,* 1967:101).

References

A. GENERAL REFERENCES

ALEMBERT, J. L. d'. *Qeuvres Complètes De d'Alembert,* IV. C. Henry, ed. Geneva: Slatkine, 1967.

BARZUN. See DIDEROT, D.
BECKER, C. L. *The Heavenly City of the Eighteenth Century Philosophers.* New Haven: Yale Univ. Press, 1969.
BECKER, H. S. *The Other Side: Perspectives on Deviance.* New York: Free Press, 1973, pp. 177-211.
——— *Outsiders: Studies In The Sociology of Deviance.* New York: Free Press, 1963.
——— "Whose Side Are We On?" *Social Problems,* Vol. 14 (Winter, 1967), No. 3, pp. 239-247.
——— "Labelling Theory Reconsidered," *Outsiders: Studies In The Sociology of Deviance.* New York: Free Press, 1973, pp. 177-211.
BERGER, B. M. "Sociology and the Intellectuals: An Analysis of a Stereotype." *Antioch Review,* XVIII (1957), pp. 275-290.
BROMBERT, V. "Toward A Portrait Of The French Intellectual," *Partisan Review,* XXVII (Summer, 1960), No. 3, pp. 480-502.

CARLYLE, T. *On Heroes, Hero-worship, and the Heroic in History,* II. London: Chapman and Hall, 1840.
CHESLER, P. *Women and Madness.* New York: Avon Books, 1972.
COSER, L. A. *Men of Ideas: A Sociologist's View.* New York: Free Press, 1970.
CRESSEY, D. R. *Other People's Money: A Study in the Social Psychology of Embezzlement.* Glencoe, Ill.: Free Press, 1953.

DIDEROT, D. *Rameau's Nephew, and other Works.* J. Barzun and R. H. Bowen, ed. Indianapolis: Bobbs-Merrill, 1964.
DUNLAP, I. *The Shock of the New: Seven Historic Exhibitions of Modern Art.* London: Weidenfeld & Nicolson, 1972.

EMERSON, R. W. "The Method of Nature," *Nature, Addresses, and Lectures.* Boston: Houghton, Mifflin, 1895.

FABIAN. See GERARD, A.

FARIS, R.E.L. "Genius And Ability," *International Encyclopedia of the Social Sciences*. Vol. 3. D. L. Sills, ed. New York: Macmillan, 1968, pp. 457-461.

――― "Sociological Causes of Genius," *American Sociological Review*. Vol. 5 (October, 1940), pp. 689-699.

FLOURENS, P. *De la raison du genie et de la folie*. Paris: Garnier, 1861.

FOUCAULT, M. *Madness And Civilization: A History of Insanity in the Age of Reason*. New York: Vintage Books, 1973.

GEIGER, T. *Aufgaben und Stellung der Intelligenz in der Gesellschaft*. Stuttgart: F. Enke, 1949.

"Genie," *Allgemeine Enzyklopädie Der Wissenschaften und Künste*. Leipzig: Brockhaus, 1854, pp. 73-99. Reprinted in Graz, Austria, 1972.

――― *Der Grosse Brockhaus*. Vol. 6. Leipzig, 1930. pp. 160-161.

GERARD, A. *An Essay On Genius* (1774). Reprinted in München: Wilhelm Fink Verlag (1966), B. Fabian, ed. (with lengthy introduction by editor).

GIBBS, J. P. "Conceptions Of Deviant Behavior: The Old And The New," *Pacific Sociological Review*. Vol. 9 (Spring, 1966), pp. 9-14.

GLASER, D. "Role Models and Differential Association," in *Deviance: The Interactionist Perspective*. E. Rubington and M. S. Weinberg, ed. New York: Macmillan, 1971. pp. 326-330.

GOODE, E. "On Behalf of Labeling Theory," *Social Problems*. Vol. 22 (June, 1975), No. 5, pp. 570-583.

GRAÑA, C. *Bohemian Versus Bourgeois: French Society and the French Man of Letters in the Nineteenth Century*. New York: Basic Books, 1964.

HAVENS, G. R. *The Age of Ideas: From Reaction to Revolution in Eighteenth-Century France*. New York: Holt, 1966.

HOFSTADTER, R. *Anti-intellectualism in American Life*. New York: A. A. Knopf, 1963.

HUSZAR, G. B. de ed. *The Intellectuals: A Controversial Portrait*. Glencoe, Ill.: Free Press, 1960.

KATZ, J. "Deviance, Charisma And Rule-Defined Behavior," *Social Problems*. (Fall, 1972), pp. 186-202.

KLAPP, O. E. *Heroes, Villains, and Fools: The Changing American Character*. Englewood Cliffs, N.J.: Prentice-Hall, 1962.

KLINEBERG, O. "Genius," *Encyclopaedia of the Social Sciences*. R. A. Seligman and A. Johnson, ed. New York: 1931, pp. 612-615.

LAING, R. D. *The Divided Self*. New York: Pantheon Books, 1969.

――― *The Politics of the Family and Other Essays*. New York: Random House, 1972.

――― and A. ESTERSON. *Sanity, Madness, and the Family*. New York: Basic Books, 1964.

LAMB, C. "The Sanity of True Genius," *The Last Essays of Elia*. VII. London: Oxford Univ. Press, 1951, pp. 704-707.

LANDAU, D. and P. F. LAZARSFELD. "Quetelet, Adolphe," *International Encyclopedia of the Social Sciences.* Vol. 13. New York: Macmillan, pp. 247-255.

LEHMAN, H. "National Differences in Creativity," *American Journal of Sociology.* Vol. 52 (May, 1947), pp. 475-488.

LEMERT, E. M. *Social Pathology: A Systematic Approach To The Theory of Sociopathic Behavior.* New York: McGraw-Hill, 1951.

――― *Human Deviance, Social Problems, and Social Control.* Englewood Cliffs, N.J.: Prentice-Hall, 1967.

LORBER, J. "Deviance As Performance: The Case of Illness," *Social Problems.* Vol. 14 (Winter, 1967), No. 3. pp. 303-310.

MATZA, D. *Delinquency and Drift.* New York: John Wiley, 1964.

MOLIÈRE (Jean Baptiste Poquelin). "Monsieur de Pourceaugnac," *The Dramatic Works of Molière.* Vol. III, trans. H. Van Laun. New York: R. Worthington, 1880.

MOREL, B. A. *Traité des Dégénérescenes, physiques, intellectuelles et morales de l'Espece humaine et des Causes qui produisent ces Variétés Maladives.* Paris: J. B. Baillière, 1857.

MORLEY. See YOUNG, E.

NETTLER, G. "A Critique of Labeling," (1974) in *The Study of Social Problems: Five Perspectives.* E. Rubington and M. S. Weinberg, ed. New York: Oxford Univ. Press, 1977.

"NORDAU, M." *Encyclopaedia Judaica.* Vol. 12. New York: Macmillan, 1971, pp. 1211-1214.

PASCAL, B. *Pensées et Opuscules.* Paris: Classiques Hachette, 1968.

PECKHAM, M. *Victorian Revolutionaries: Speculations on Some Heroes of a Culture Crisis.* New York: Braziller, 1970.

POLSKY, N. *Hustlers, Beats and Others.* Middlesex, England, 1971.

PRAZ, M. *The Romantic Agony.* New York: Oxford Univ. Press. 1951.

RINGER, F. K. *The Decline of the German Mandarin.* Cambridge, Mass.: Harvard Univ. Press, 1969.

ROSEN, G. *Madness In Society: Chapters in the Historical Sociology of Mental Illness.* New York: Harper & Row, 1969.

RUBINGTON, E. and M. S. WEINBERG. *Deviance: The Interactionist Perspective.* London: Macmillan, 1971.

SAINT-SIMON, H. de. "Letters From An Inhabitant Of Geneva To His Contemporaries," (1803) in *Social Organization, The Science Of Man And Other Writings.* F. Markham, ed. New York: Harper and Row, 1964.

SCHEFF, T. J. ed. *Mental Illness and Social Processes.* New York: Harper and Row, 1967.

SCHEFF, T. J. "Negotiating Reality: Notes On Power In The Assessment Of Responsibility," *Social Problems*. Vol. 16 (Summer, 1968), pp. 3-17.
——— *Being Mentally Ill: A Sociological Theory*. Chicago: Aldine, 1974.
SCHUR, E. M. *Labeling Deviant Behavior: Its Sociological Implications*. New York: Harper and Row, 1971.
SEEMAN, M. "The Intellectual And The Language Of Minorities," *American Journal of Sociology*. LXIV (July, 1958), No. 1, pp. 25-35.
SYKES, G. M. and D. MATZA. "Techniques of Neutralization: A Theory of Delinquency," *American Sociological Review*, Vol. 22 (December, 1957), pp. 667-670.
SZASZ, T. S. *The Myth of Mental Illness*. New York: Dell, 1961.
——— "The Psychiatrist As Double Agent," *Trans-action*. (October, 1967), pp. 16-24.
——— *The Manufacture Of Madness*. New York: Dell, 1970.

TOCQUEVILLE, A. de. "How Towards the Middle of the Eighteenth Century Men of Letters Took the Lead in Politics and the Consequences of this New Development," in *The Intellectuals: A Controversial Portrait*. G. B. de Huszar, ed. Glencoe, Ill.: Free Press, 1970.
TONELLI, G. "Genius From The Renaissance To 1770," *Dictionary of the History of Ideas*. P. P. Wiener, ed. New York: Scribners, 1973, pp. 293-298.
TRILLING, L. *The Liberal Imagination: Essays On Literature and Society*. New York: Viking Press, 1950.
TUKE, D. H. *Insanity In Ancient And Modern Life*. London: Macmillan, 1878.

VOLTAIRE, F. "Imagination," in *The Works of Voltaire*. Vol. VI. New York: E. R. De Mont, 1901, pp. 155-171.

WILLIAMS, C. J. and M. S. WEINBERG. *Homosexuals and the Military: A Study of Less than Honorable Discharge*. New York: Harper and Row, 1971.
WILSON, E. *The Wound And The Bow*. Boston: Houghton Mifflin, 1941.
WITTKOWER, R. "Genius: Individualism In Art And Artists," *Dictionary of the History of Ideas*. P. P. Wiener, ed. New York: Scribners, 1973, pp. 297-312.
——— and M. WITTKOWER. *Born Under Saturn*. London: Shenval Press Limited, 1963.

YOUNG, E. *Conjectures On Original Composition* (1759). Reprinted in London: Longmans, Green & Co., 1918, E. Morley, ed. (with introduction by editor).

B. LIST OF SAMPLE POPULATION

Anonymous. "Reason, Genius, And Madness," *Medical Critic And Psychological Journal*, Vol. I, 1861, pp. 132-142.
ARMSTRONG-JONES, R. "The Relation Of Genius To Insanity," *The Sociological Review*. Vol. VII. London: Sherratt and Hughes, 1914, pp. 156-163.

AUERBACK, A. "Uber Lombroso's Auffassung des Genies," *Deutsche Medizinal-Zeitung.* No. 35 (April 29, 1895), pp. 383-386.

BABCOCK, W. L. "On The Morbid Heredity And Predisposition To Insanity Of The Man Of Genius," *The Journal Of Nervous And Mental Disease.* Vol. XX (December, 1895), No. 12, pp. 749-769.

BAISCH, H. "Wahrsinn oder Wahnsinn des Genius?" *Beihefte zur Zeitschrift für angewandte Psychologie und Charakterkunde.* No. 85. Leipzig: Johann Ambrosius Barth, 1939, pp. 1-79.

BOWERMANN, W. G. *Studies In Genius.* New York: Philosophical Library, 1947.

BURKS, B. S., et al. *The Promise Of Youth: Follow-Up Studies Of A Thousand Gifted Children.* Vol. III of *Genetic Studies Of Genius.* Stanford: Stanford Univ. Press (1930), 1961.

CAHAN, J. *Zur Kritik des Geniebegriffs.* Bern: Scheitlin and Co., 1911.

CARROLL, H. A. *Genius In The Making.* New York: McGraw-Hill, 1940.

CONSTABLE, F. C. *Poverty And Hereditary Genius: A Criticism Of Mr. Francis Galton's Theory Of Hereditary Genius.* London: Arthur C. Fifield, 1905.

COOLEY, C. H. "Genius, Fame And The Comparison Of Races," *Annals Of The American Academy Of Political And Social Science.* May, 1897, pp. 317-358.

COX, C. M. *The Early Mental Traits Of Three Hundred Geniuses.* Vol. II of *Genetic Studies Of Genius,* Stanford: Stanford Univ. Press, (1926), 1959.

DILTHEY, W. *Dichterische Einbildungskraft Und Wahnsinn.* Leipzig: Duncker and Humblot, 1886.

ELLIS, H. *A Study Of British Genius.* London: Constable and Company Limited (1904), 1927.

FREUD, S. "Leonardo Da Vinci And A Memory Of His Childhood" (1910), *The Standard Edition Of The Complete Psychological Works Of Sigmund Freud.* Vol. XI. London: Hogarth Press and the Institute Of Psycho-Analysis, 1957.
——— "The Relation Of The Poet To Day-Dreaming" (1908), *Sigmund Freud: On Creativity And The Unconscious.* New York: Harper and Row, 1958.

GALTON, F. *Hereditary Genius: An Inquiry into Its Laws and Consequences* (1869). Cleveland: Meridian Books, World Publishing Co., 1962.

HAGEN, F. W. "Ueber die Verwandtschaft des Genies mit dem Irresein," *Allgemeine Zeitschrift Für Psychiatrie Und Ihre Grenzgebiete,* 1877, pp. 640-675.

HINKLE, B. M. *The Re-Creating Of The Individual.* New York: Harcourt, Brace, 1923.

HIRSCH, N.D.M. *Genius And Creative Intelligence.* Cambridge, Mass.: Sci-Art Publishers, 1931.

HIRSCH, W. *Genius And Degeneration: A Psychological Study.* London: William Heinemann, 1897.

HOCK, A. *Die methodische Entwicklung der Talente und des Genies.* Leipzig: Akademische Verlagsgesellschaft, 1920.

——— *The Origin Of Genius.* Trans. from the German by J. Gutman. Binghamton, N.Y.: the author, 1949.

HOESCH-ERNST, L. *Das Jugendliche Genie: Anthropologisch-Psychologische Studie.* Geneva: 1909.

HOFFMANN, R. A. "Kant und Swedenborg," *Grenzfragen Des Nerven-Und Seelenlebens.* Vol. 69. Wiesbaden: J. F. Bergmann, 1909, pp. 1-29.

HOLLINGWORTH, L. A. *Gifted Children: Their Nature And Nurture.* New York: Macmillan, 1926.

HYSLOP, T. B. *The Great Abnormals.* New York: George H. Doran Co., 1925.

JACOBSON, A. C. *Genius: Some Revaluations.* New York: Greenberg Publishers, 1926.

JASPERS, K. "Strindberg Und Van Gogh," *Philosophische Forschungen.* No. 3. Berlin: Julius Springer, 1926.

JSENBURG, W. K. *Genie und Landschaft im europäischen Raum.* Berlin: J. A. Stargardt, 1936.

KARPATH, L. *Begegnung Mit Dem Genius.* Vienna: Fiba Verlag, 1934.

KOLLER, A. H. *The Abbé Du Bos-His Advocacy Of The Theory Of Climate.* Champaign, Ill.: Garrard Press, 1937.

KRETSCHMER, E. *The Psychology Of Men Of Genius.* New York: Harcourt, Brace, 1931.

LANGE-EICHBAUM, W. *Genie-Irrsin Und Ruhm.* Munich: Ernst Reinhardt (1927), 1935.

——— *The Problem Of Genius.* New York: Macmillan (1930), 1932.

LÉLUT, L.-F. *Du Demon de Socrate.* Paris: Trinquart, Libraire-Editeur, 1836.

——— *L'Amulette De Pascal.* Paris: Chez J.-B. Bailliere, 1846.

LOMBROSO, C. *The Man Of Genius* (1863). New York: Scribners, 1891.

MacDONALD, A. "Genius and Insanity," *The Journal Of Mental Science.* Vol. 38 (April, 1892), pp. 186-195.

MARKS, J. *Genius and Disaster: Studies in Drugs and Genius.* New York: Adelphi, 1926.

MAUDSLEY, H. "Heredity In Health And Disease," *The Fortnightly Review.* Vol. XXXIX (May, 1886), London, pp. 648-659.

——— *Heredity, Variation And Genius.* London: John Bale, Sons and Danielsson, Ltd., 1908.

MÖBIUS, P. J. "Ueber das Studium der Talente," *Zeitschrift für Hypnotismus.* Vol. X, 1902, pp. 5, 66-74.

——— *Geothe.* Vol. I and II of *Ausgewählte Werke.* Leipzig: Johan Ambrosius Barth, 1909.

MOORMAN, L. J. *Tuberculosis and Genius.* Chicago: Univ. of Chicago Press, 1940.

MOREAU, J.-J. *La Psychologie morbide dans ses rapports avec la philosophie de l'histoire.* Paris: V. Masson, 1859.

NISBET, J. F. *The Insanity of Genius: And the General Inequality of Human Faculty Physiologically Considered* (1891). London: Stanley Paul, 1912.
NOACK, L. "Dichterwahnsinn und wahnsinnige Dichter," *Psyche.* Vol. 2, 1859, p. 247-264.
NORDAU, M. *Degeneration* (1892). New York: D. Appleton, 1900.

ODEN. See TERMAN, L.

PADOVAN, A. *The Sons Of Glory: Studies In Genius.* London: T. Fischer Unwin, 1902.

RADESTOCK, P. *Genie Und Wahnsinn: Eine Psychologische Untersuchung.* Breslau: E. Trewendt, 1884.
RHODES, H.T.F. *Genius And Criminal: A Study In Rebellion.* London: John Murray, 1932.
ROYSE, N. K. *A Study Of Genius.* Chicago: Rand, McNally, 1891.

SADGER, J. "Heinrich von Kleist: Eine pathographisch-psychologische Studie," *Grenzfragen des Nerven-und Seelenlebens.* Vol. 70. Wiesbaden: J. F. Bergmann, 1910, pp. 1-63.
SANBORN, K. *The Vanity And Insanity Of Genius.* New York: Georg J. Coombes, 1886.
SCHILLING, J. A. *Psychiatrische Briefe.* Augsburg: J. A. Schlosser (1863), 1866.
SCHWARZ, O. L. *General Types Of Superior Men.* Boston: Richard G. Badger, 1916.
SHAW, B. *The Sanity of Art* (1895). New York: B. R. Tucker, 1908.
STEKEL, W. "Dichtung und Neurose," *Grenzfragen Des Nerven-und Seelenlebens.* Bol. 65. Wiesbaden: J. F. Bergmann, 1909.
――― "Nietzsche und Wagner: Eine Sexualpsychologische Studie zur Psychogenese des Freundschaftsgefühles und des Freundschaftsverrates," *Zeitschrift für Sexualwissenschaft und Sexualpolitik.* Vol. 4. 1917, pp. 22-28, 58-65.
STEVENSON, W. G. "Genius And Mental Disease," *The Popular Science Monthly.* Vol. XXX. New York, (March, 1887) pp. 663-678.
SULLY, J. "Genius And Insanity," *The Nineteenth Century.* Vol. XVII (June, 1885), pp. 948-969;

TERMAN, L. M. et al. *Mental And Psychological Traits Of A Thousand Gifted Children.* Vol. I of *Genetic Studies Of Genius.* Stanford: Stanford Univ. Press (1925), 1959.
TERMAN, L. M. and M. H. ODEN, et al. *The Gifted Child Grows Up: Twenty-Five Years' Follow-Up Of A Superior Group.* Vol. IV of *Genetic Studies Of Genius.* Stanford: Stanford Univ. Press (1947), 1959.
TOULOUSE, É. *Enquête Médico-Psychologique Sur Les Rapports De La Supériorité Intellectuelle Ave La Névropathie.* Paris: Société D'Editions Scientifiques, 1896.

TSANOFF, R. A. *The Ways of Genius.* New York: Harper and Brothers, 1949.
TÜRCK, H. *The Man Of Genius* (1896). Schwerin: Stillersche Hofbuchhandlung (J. A. Strange), 1914.

WALSHE, W. H. *The Colloquial Faculty For Languages: Cerebral Localization And The Nature Of Genius.* London: J. and A. Churchill, 1886.
WARD, L. F. *Applied Sociology: A Treatise On The Conscious Improvement Of Society By Society.* Boston: Ginn and Co., 1906.

ZILSEL, E. *Die Geniereligion.* Vienna: Wilhelm Braumüller, 1918.
––– *Die Entstehung Des Geniebegriffes.* Tübingen: J.C.B. Mohr (Paul Siebeck), 1926.

Index

Index

"Quarrel of Ancients and Moderns," 108
Quételet, A., 88, 103

Radestock, P., 52n, 83n
Realism, 40, 105n, 114
Reason (see Genius, and judgment)
Rhodes, H., 44, 111
Ringer, F., 123n
Romantics, 32n-33n, 55, 73-74, 128
  and originality, 69, 74n
  redefinition of genius, 13, 26-28, 31, 55, 60, 64, 68-70, 71, 76, 109
  and self-labeling, 55-56, 127
  "Sturm und Drang," 66n
  and "Weltschmerz," 66n
Rosen, G., 76, 124n
Royse, N. K., 37-38, 52n, 113-114, 122n
Rubington, E., 132n
Rush, B., 93, 105n

Sadger, J., 106n
Saint-Simon, H. de, 57
Sanborn, K., 70-71
Scheff, T., 14-15, 19n, 133n
Schelling, F. W. v., 27
Schiller, F. v., 27, 68-69, 71
Schlegel brothers, 27, 68-69
Schopenhauer, A., 27, 56, 59, 76
Schur, E., 129
Schwarz, O., 40, 59-60, 103n, 122n
Seeman, M., 33n
Shakespeare, W., 71
Shaw, G. B., 29, 53n, 97, 110
Shelley, P. B., 67
Social control (see Labeling, and social control)
Social control model, 19n (see also Labeling, perspective)
Social reaction model, 19n (see also Labeling, perspective)

Social system model, 14-15 (see also Scheff, T.)
Socrates, 22, 28
Stekel, W., 29, 45, 47, 53n, 80
Stevenson, W. G., 53n, 65, 71-72
"Sturm und Drang," 33n
Sully, J., 52n, 65
Swedenborg, E., 58
Swift, J., 67
Sykes, G. M., 133n
Symbolic interactionism, 129
Szasz, T., 120-121, 123n-124n

Talent (see Genius, and talent)
Terman, L., 29, 46, 62
Tocqueville, A. de, 118
Tolstoy, L. N., 122n
Toulouse, E., 36, 52n-53n, 73
Tsanoff, R. A., 41, 52n
Türck, H., 59
Tuke, D., 96, 105n

Vasari, 31n
Vinci, L. da, 71
Virchow, R., 94-95
Voltaire, F., 25, 76, 82n

Ward, L., 62
Weinberg, M. S., 132n-133n
"Weltschmerz," 66n, 67, 128
Wieland, C., 56, 58
Will (volition), 75-78, 81, 82n-83n
  and genius, 81, 83n, 112
Williams, C. J., 133n
Wilson, E., 52n
Wittkower, M., 23
Wittkower, R., 23, 26, 32n, 74n

Young, E., 32n

Zilsel, E., 31n, 122n
Zola, E., 29, 52n, 72-73

About the Author

Dr. George Becker is an Assistant Professor of Sociology at Vanderbilt University. His major research and teaching interests are the family, deviance, theory and historical sociology. He has earned his Ph.D. in sociology in 1976 from the State University of New York at Stony Brook and holds degrees in education and modern European history. Dr. Becker's current research deals with the rise of the modern intellectual during the seventeenth and eighteenth centuries.